The Window of Tolerance Parenting

Evidence-Based Nervous System Tools to Keep Kids in the Green Zone from Toddlers to Teens

Vicki Katrina

First edition, 2025

ISBN (paperback): **978-1-923604-20-9**
ISBN (eBook): **978-1-923604-21-6**

This book provides general information and practical strategies for parents and carers. It is **not medical, psychological, legal, or educational advice**, and it is **not a substitute** for care from a qualified professional. Always seek the advice of your GP, paediatrician, or a licensed mental health professional regarding your child's specific needs. If you are concerned about safety or risk of harm, contact **emergency services** immediately.

References to clinicians, researchers, frameworks, and publishers (for example, **Daniel J. Siegel**, **Stephen W. Porges**, **Bessel A. van der Kolk**, **Marsha M. Linehan**, **John Gottman**, and others) are provided for **educational citation** only. This work is **independent** and **not affiliated with, sponsored by, or endorsed by** any person or organisation named. The term **"window of tolerance"** is used **descriptively** to refer to a concept in the clinical literature.

All product names, brands, and trademarks remain the property of their respective owners. Use in this book is **descriptive** and **does not imply endorsement**.

Any stories, names, or examples are **composites** or have been **anonymised**. Any resemblance to actual persons, living or dead, is **coincidental**.

Every child is different. Adapt suggestions to your child's age, development, culture, and context. The author and publisher disclaim liability for any loss or harm arising from the use of the information contained herein.

Table of Contents

Chapter 1: The Window of Tolerance

A New Lens for Understanding Your Child

Jessica stared at her kitchen table, bewildered. Her seven-year-old son Jake was having a complete meltdown over his math homework—tears streaming down his face, pencil thrown across the room, papers scattered everywhere. Meanwhile, just ten feet away in the living room, her four-year-old daughter Emma sat peacefully watching cartoons, completely unaffected by the chaos.

Same house. Same afternoon. Same family stress levels. Yet two completely different responses.

Sound familiar? You've probably witnessed scenes like this countless times, wondering why one child can roll with life's punches while another seems to fall apart at the slightest challenge. The answer isn't about one child being "stronger" or "more sensitive" than the other. It's about something far more fascinating and actionable: their **window of tolerance**.

Understanding the Window of Tolerance

The window of tolerance is a concept developed by Dr. Dan Siegel, a clinical psychiatry professor at UCLA and one of the world's leading researchers on how the brain develops. Simply put, it's the zone where your child can handle life's ups and downs while staying regulated, connected, and able to think clearly (Siegel, 2012).

Think of it like your child's emotional thermostat. Just like a thermostat keeps your house at a comfortable temperature, your child's nervous system tries to keep them in a zone where they can learn, play, connect, and cope. When they're in this sweet spot—their window of tolerance—they can handle challenges, make good choices, and bounce back from disappointments.

But here's where it gets interesting. That window isn't the same size for every child, and it's not even the same size for the same child on different days. Jake's window might be naturally narrower than Emma's, or maybe his homework triggered something that temporarily shrunk his ability to cope.

The Three Zones of Your Child's Nervous System

Your child's nervous system operates in three distinct zones, each with its own characteristics and behaviors:

The Green Zone (Optimal Arousal) When your child is in their window of tolerance, they're in what we call the green zone. This is where the magic happens. Their prefrontal cortex—the thinking, reasoning part of their brain—is online and working well. They can:

- Listen and follow directions

- Problem-solve creatively

- Show empathy for others

- Learn new information

- Regulate their emotions

- Connect meaningfully with family members

In the green zone, your child feels safe, calm, and alert. They might still feel emotions—excitement, disappointment, frustration—but these feelings don't overwhelm their system.

The Red Zone (Hyperarousal) When stress, excitement, or overwhelm pushes your child above their window of tolerance, they enter the red zone. Their nervous system goes into fight-or-flight mode. You might see:

- Tantrums, meltdowns, or explosive anger

- Hyperactivity or inability to sit still

- Defiance or aggressive behavior

- Racing thoughts or rapid speech

- Anxiety or panic responses

- Physical symptoms like headaches or stomachaches

Children in the red zone aren't choosing to be difficult. Their nervous system has detected a threat (real or perceived) and activated their survival responses. The thinking brain goes offline, and the emotional brain takes over.

The Blue Zone (Hypoarousal) When your child drops below their window of tolerance, they enter the blue zone. This is the nervous system's shutdown response. You might notice:

- Withdrawal or seeming "checked out"

- Extreme tiredness or lethargy

- Difficulty concentrating or remembering

- Appearing "spacey" or disconnected

- Regression to younger behaviors

- Physical complaints without clear cause

Children in the blue zone might look calm on the outside, but internally they've disconnected to protect themselves from overwhelm. This isn't laziness or defiance—it's their nervous system's way of conserving energy when it feels depleted or threatened.

Your Child's Emotional Thermostat

Picture your child's nervous system as a thermostat that's constantly monitoring their internal and external environment. Just like a home thermostat kicks on the heat when it's too cold or the air conditioning when it's too hot, your child's nervous system activates different responses based on what it perceives.

But unlike your home thermostat, which you can set to exactly 72 degrees, your child's "thermostat" is influenced by countless factors:

- Their individual temperament

- How much sleep they got last night

- What they ate for breakfast

- The noise level in their environment

- Upcoming changes or transitions

- Past experiences and memories

- Your own emotional state

- Peer interactions at school

This is why the same child who handles a busy morning routine beautifully on Tuesday might completely fall apart on Wednesday when faced with the exact same tasks. Their window of tolerance shifted based on these variable factors.

Why Windows Vary So Much

Understanding that windows of tolerance are highly individual helps explain so many parenting mysteries. Emma's naturally wide window allows her to stay regulated even when there's chaos around her. Jake's narrower window means he needs more support to stay in his green zone, especially when faced with challenges like homework.

Temperament plays a huge role. Some children are born with more sensitive nervous systems—they notice more, feel more deeply, and get overwhelmed more easily. Others have robust systems that can handle lots of stimulation without getting knocked out of their window. Neither is better or worse; they're just different starting points.

Daily variables constantly affect window size. A child who typically has a decent-sized window might wake up with a much smaller one if they:

- Didn't sleep well

- Are fighting off a cold

- Had a conflict with a friend at school

- Are worried about an upcoming test

- Experienced a change in routine

Think of these factors as either expanding or contracting your child's window moment by moment throughout the day.

When Traditional Discipline Backfires

Here's where this concept becomes revolutionary for parenting. Traditional discipline approaches often assume that children are making conscious choices about their behavior. Time-outs, consequences, and punishment all rely on the prefrontal cortex being online and available for learning.

But when your child is outside their window of tolerance—whether in the red zone or blue zone—their thinking brain is essentially offline. Asking a dysregulated child to "think about what they did wrong" is like asking someone having a panic attack to solve a math problem. The brain simply isn't available for that kind of processing.

This explains why consequences often seem to make behavior worse rather than better. A child in the red zone who gets sent to time-out might escalate further because isolation feels threatening to a nervous system already in survival mode. A child in the blue zone might comply with punishment but not actually learn anything because their brain has checked out.

Window-aware responses, on the other hand, focus first on helping your child return to their green zone where learning and connection can happen. Once they're regulated, then you can address the behavior, problem-solve together, and establish expectations for next time.

The Neuroscience Made Simple

You don't need a PhD in neuroscience to understand what's happening in your child's brain, but knowing the basics helps everything else make sense.

Your child has essentially two brain systems that matter most for regulation:

The Limbic System (Emotional Brain) This ancient part of the brain is designed for survival. It's always scanning for threats and ready to activate fight, flight, or freeze responses. It processes information lightning-fast but not very accurately—it would rather mistake a stick for a snake than miss a real danger.

The limbic system includes the amygdala, which acts like a smoke detector. When it perceives a threat (physical, emotional, or social), it sets off alarms that flood the body with stress hormones and prepare for immediate action.

The Prefrontal Cortex (Thinking Brain)
This newer part of the brain handles executive functions like planning, problem-solving, impulse control, and emotional regulation. It's slower than the limbic system but much more accurate and sophisticated.

The prefrontal cortex doesn't fully mature until around age 25, which means children and teenagers are naturally more reactive and have less self-control than adults.

Here's the crucial part: **when the limbic system is activated, it essentially hijacks the prefrontal cortex**. Blood flow and glucose get redirected to support the survival response, leaving less resources available for thinking and reasoning.

This is why a child who can normally solve problems, show empathy, and control their impulses might suddenly seem incapable of any of these skills when they're dysregulated. Their brain has temporarily prioritized survival over thinking.

Practical Assessment: Identifying Your Child's Window Patterns

Understanding your individual child's window patterns is the first step toward supporting their regulation. Every child has unique triggers, warning signs, and recovery needs.

Recognizing Green Zone Signs:

- Follows instructions without major resistance
- Shows curiosity and asks questions
- Plays cooperatively with siblings
- Handles minor disappointments without major reactions
- Makes eye contact and engages in conversation
- Shows empathy when others are upset
- Can transition between activities with minimal support

Red Zone Warning Signs:

- Voice gets louder or higher-pitched
- Movement becomes more rapid or jerky
- Difficulty following simple directions
- Increased impulsivity or risk-taking
- Physical aggression toward people or objects
- Rapid mood swings
- Complaints of feeling hot, headaches, or stomachaches

Blue Zone Indicators:

- Seems "foggy" or disconnected
- Responds slowly or not at all to questions
- Decreased physical activity or energy
- Regression to younger behaviors (baby talk, clinginess)

- Difficulty making simple decisions

- Appears sad or withdrawn without clear reason

- Physical complaints like tiredness or feeling cold

Tracking Patterns Over Time: Keep a simple log for a week, noting:

- Time of day when dysregulation typically occurs

- What was happening right before (transitions, demands, conflicts)

- How long episodes lasted

- What helped (or didn't help) with recovery

- Environmental factors (noise, crowds, hunger, tiredness)

You'll likely start seeing patterns that help you predict and prevent window exits.

Family Window Mapping Exercise

Since everyone in your family has their own window of tolerance, and these windows affect each other, it's helpful to map out your family's regulation patterns.

Create a simple chart with columns for:

- Each family member's name

- Typical green zone behaviors

- Red zone triggers and signs

- Blue zone triggers and signs

- What helps each person return to green

Notice the connections:

- Does one person's red zone trigger another family member's dysregulation?

- Are there times of day when multiple people struggle?

- Which family member's regulation most affects the others?

- What environmental factors impact the whole family's windows?

This mapping helps you understand your family as a regulation system rather than just individual people trying to manage their own emotions.

Before and After: Window-Aware Responses in Action

Traditional Response to Jake's Homework Meltdown: "Jake, you need to calm down right now. This behavior is unacceptable. If you don't stop crying and get back to your homework, you're going to lose screen time tonight. You're seven years old—you should be able to handle simple math problems without falling apart."

Window-Aware Response: "Oh buddy, I can see your nervous system is really activated right now. Let's take a break from homework and help your body calm down. Come sit with me and we'll do some deep breathing together. Once you're feeling more settled, we can figure out a way to make this math feel less overwhelming."

The difference? The traditional response demands that Jake use his prefrontal cortex (thinking brain) when it's offline due to stress. The window-aware response recognizes his nervous system state and prioritizes regulation first.

Traditional Response to Blue Zone Behavior: "Emma, you're being lazy. I asked you three times to put your backpack away. If I have to ask again, you're going to your room. Other kids your age don't need constant reminders."

Window-Aware Response: "Emma, I notice you seem pretty tired and disconnected right now. Let me help you with your backpack, and then let's see if we can figure out what your body needs to feel more awake and present. Maybe some water or a quick movement break?"

Again, the window-aware approach recognizes the nervous system state rather than interpreting the behavior as willful non-compliance.

The Ripple Effect of Window Awareness

When you start responding to your child's behavior through the lens of nervous system regulation rather than compliance and control, everything begins to shift. Children feel understood rather than criticized. They learn to recognize their own internal states. Most importantly, they experience their parent as a source of co-regulation rather than an additional stressor.

This doesn't mean permissiveness or avoiding boundaries. It means **timing** your guidance and expectations for when your child's brain is actually available to receive them. It means distinguishing between a child who won't listen and a child who can't listen due to their nervous system state.

Over time, children who receive window-aware parenting develop:

- Better emotional vocabulary and self-awareness
- Increased ability to communicate their needs
- More effective self-regulation strategies
- Stronger trust in their parents' support
- Greater resilience in facing challenges

Moving Forward with Window Awareness

Understanding the window of tolerance gives you a completely new framework for interpreting your child's behavior and responding in ways that build their capacity for regulation rather than demanding it.

In Jake's case, Jessica learned to recognize the signs that his window was narrowing—the fidgeting, the complaints about homework being "stupid," the increasingly frustrated sighs. Instead of pushing through, she started offering regulation support: a quick walk around the block, some deep breathing exercises, or breaking the work into smaller chunks.

For Emma, Jessica realized that what looked like defiance was often her nervous system in shutdown mode. A gentle touch, some engaging conversation, or invitation to movement helped bring Emma back online much more effectively than consequences or criticism.

The window of tolerance isn't just a concept—it's a practical tool that transforms how you understand and respond to your child's most challenging moments. When you can see past the surface behavior to the nervous system state underneath, you become your child's ally in regulation rather than their opponent in a power struggle.

Essential Points to Remember:

- **Every child has a unique window of tolerance that changes based on daily variables**

- **Behavior outside the window isn't a choice—it's a nervous system response**

- **The goal is regulation first, then teaching and problem-solving**

- **Your own regulation directly impacts your child's ability to stay in their window**

- **Window-aware parenting builds capacity rather than demanding compliance**

As we move forward in this book, you'll learn specific strategies for supporting your child's regulation, expanding their window over time, and creating a family environment where everyone's nervous system can thrive. The window of tolerance isn't just about managing difficult behavior—it's about raising children who understand themselves, trust their support system, and develop the resilience to navigate life's inevitable challenges.

Chapter 2: The Science of Co-Regulation

Your Nervous System as Your Child's GPS

Marcus watched his two-year-old daughter Lily's face scrunch up in that all-too-familiar way. They were in the cereal aisle at the grocery store, and she'd just spotted the colorful cartoon characters on the sugar-laden boxes she wasn't allowed to have. Here it comes, he thought.

But instead of tensing up or launching into his usual "No, we're not buying that" lecture, Marcus took a slow, deep breath. He crouched down to Lily's level, keeping his voice calm and steady. "I see you really want that cereal. Those characters look pretty exciting, don't they?"

Lily's building whimper paused. She looked at her dad's relaxed face, felt his unhurried energy. Something in her little nervous system seemed to settle. Instead of the full meltdown Marcus had been bracing for, she simply nodded and pointed to their cart. "Want our cereal?"

"Yes, we have our cereal right here," Marcus confirmed gently. "Good remembering."

As they walked toward checkout, Marcus marveled at what had just happened. Six months ago, this same scenario would have ended with Lily screaming on the floor while he felt his own stress skyrocket, creating a feedback loop that took both of them twenty minutes to recover from.

The difference wasn't that Lily had suddenly become more mature or compliant. The difference was Marcus's nervous system—and how it directly influenced hers.

Your Nervous System Is Contagious

Here's something that might surprise you: **your child's ability to stay regulated depends more on your nervous system than on their own willpower**. This isn't about being a "perfect" parent or never feeling stressed. It's about understanding how your internal state directly transmits to your child and learning to work with this biological reality rather than against it.

The scientific term for this phenomenon is *co-regulation*—the process by which one person's regulated nervous system helps another person's dysregulated system return to balance (Siegel, 2020). Think of it like having emotional Wi-Fi that's always broadcasting your internal state to everyone around you, especially your children.

Children under age five have virtually no capacity for independent emotional regulation. Their nervous systems are designed to sync up with their caregivers for survival. Even older children and teenagers continue to rely heavily on co-regulation from trusted adults, though they develop increasing ability to self-regulate as their brains mature.

This means that when you're trying to calm down an upset child while your own nervous system is activated—heart racing, jaw clenched, thoughts spinning—you're essentially trying to put out a fire while pouring gasoline on it.

The Three-Level Nervous System Response

To understand how co-regulation works, you need to know about the three levels of your nervous system response, based on Dr. Stephen Porges' groundbreaking polyvagal theory (Porges, 2011). These three systems developed over millions of years of evolution and activate in a specific hierarchy when we face challenges.

Level 1: Social Engagement System (Newest) This is your most sophisticated nervous system response, located in the newest part of your brain. When this system is online, you feel:

- Safe and connected

- Curious and playful

- Able to communicate clearly

- Capable of creative problem-solving

- Naturally warm and empathetic

Your face is relaxed, your voice has natural melody and rhythm, and your body language invites connection. This is the state where co-regulation happens most effectively.

Level 2: Sympathetic Fight-or-Flight (Middle) When your social engagement system goes offline due to perceived threat, your sympathetic nervous system activates. You might experience:

- Increased heart rate and breathing

- Muscle tension and restlessness

- Racing thoughts or difficulty concentrating

- Urges to argue, control, or escape

- Feeling overwhelmed or panicked

Your voice becomes flatter or sharper, your face loses expressiveness, and your body language signals danger to others—including your child.

Level 3: Dorsal Vagal Shutdown (Oldest) If the fight-or-flight response doesn't resolve the threat, your oldest nervous system response kicks in—shutdown or freeze. You might notice:

- Feeling numb or disconnected

- Extreme fatigue or brain fog

- Difficulty making decisions

- Wanting to withdraw or hide

- Sense of hopelessness or depression

Your face becomes mask-like, your voice loses energy, and you may seem physically present but emotionally unavailable.

Here's the crucial part: **your child's nervous system is constantly reading and responding to which level you're operating from**. When you're in social engagement, your child's system naturally gravitates toward regulation. When you drop into fight-or-flight or shutdown, your child's system often follows.

Mirror Neurons and Emotional Contagion

The biological mechanism behind co-regulation involves specialized brain cells called *mirror neurons*. These cells fire both when you perform an action and when you observe someone else performing the same action (Rizzolatti & Craighero, 2004). They're part of why you might automatically smile when someone smiles at you, or why you feel tense when you're around an anxious person.

Mirror neurons help explain emotional contagion—the phenomenon where emotions literally spread from person to person through unconscious mimicry of facial expressions, body language, and vocal tones. Your child's mirror neurons are constantly firing in response to your emotional state, creating neural pathways that match your internal experience.

This is why a parent's genuine calm can be more effective than any parenting technique. Your child's brain is literally downloading your nervous system state and using it as a template for their own regulation.

But here's what makes it even more powerful: children's mirror neuron systems are hyperactive compared to adults'. They're biologically designed to sync up with their caregivers for survival. This means your emotional state has an outsized impact on your child's nervous system, especially during times of stress or uncertainty.

The Biology of Connection

The co-regulation process involves specific hormones and neurotransmitters that either support connection or create distance between you and your child.

Oxytocin: The Connection Chemical When you're in a regulated state and responding to your child with warmth and presence, your brain releases oxytocin—often called the "love hormone" or "bonding hormone" (Carter, 2014). This powerful neurochemical:

- Reduces cortisol (stress hormone) levels

- Increases feelings of trust and safety

- Enhances emotional attunement between parent and child

- Strengthens neural pathways associated with secure attachment

The beautiful thing about oxytocin is that it's contagious. When your brain releases it, your child's brain tends to follow suit, creating a positive feedback loop of connection and regulation.

Cortisol: The Stress Disruptor When you're dysregulated—whether in fight-or-flight or shutdown mode—your body produces cortisol. While cortisol serves important functions in small doses, chronic elevation can (Gunnar & Quevedo, 2007):

- Impair memory and learning

- Weaken immune system function

- Disrupt sleep and appetite

- Interfere with emotional regulation

- Damage developing brain architecture in children

Children's cortisol levels mirror their parents' patterns. A chronically stressed parent often has a chronically stressed child, creating a cycle that affects the whole family's health and well-being.

The Attachment Security Loop Secure attachment develops when children consistently experience their caregivers as safe harbors during times of distress (Bowlby, 1988). This happens through thousands of small co-regulation moments where:

1. Child becomes dysregulated

2. Parent remains calm and present

3. Parent offers attuned support

4. Child's nervous system settles

5. Connection is restored and strengthened

Over time, these experiences literally shape your child's developing brain, creating neural pathways that support emotional resilience, healthy relationships, and stress management throughout their life.

How Your Regulation Affects Your Child's Regulation

The impact of your nervous system state on your child goes far beyond momentary co-regulation. Your baseline level of regulation— how you typically handle stress, express emotions, and manage relationships—becomes your child's template for normal.

Modeling Self-Regulation Skills Children learn emotional regulation not through lectures or consequences, but by observing how the important adults in their life handle challenging situations. When you:

- Take deep breaths when frustrated

- Ask for help when overwhelmed

- Take breaks when you need them

- Express emotions without losing control

- Repair relationships after conflicts

Your child's brain is recording these patterns and developing similar neural pathways. You're literally teaching them how to be human through your own nervous system management.

Creating Safety Through Predictability A regulated parent is a predictable parent. When your child can generally anticipate your responses—knowing that you'll stay calm during their storms, that you'll follow through on commitments, that you won't suddenly explode or withdraw—their nervous system can relax.

This predictability allows children to use their energy for learning and growing rather than constantly scanning for signs of danger in their environment.

The Ripple Effect on Family Systems Your regulation status affects not just your relationship with each individual child, but the entire family dynamic. A regulated parent:

- Makes decisions from a place of clarity rather than reactivity

- Sets boundaries with warmth rather than anger

- Handles sibling conflicts without taking sides

- Creates routines that support everyone's nervous system

- Models healthy stress management for the whole family

Breaking Intergenerational Patterns of Dysregulation

One of the most powerful aspects of understanding co-regulation is realizing that you have the opportunity to break cycles of dysregulation that may have been passed down through generations in your family.

Many adults grew up with parents who, despite their best intentions, operated from chronic fight-or-flight or shutdown states due to their own unresolved trauma, stress, or lack of support. These parents may have:

- Yelled frequently when overwhelmed

- Withdrawn emotionally during conflicts
- Used harsh punishments when dysregulated
- Created chaotic or unpredictable home environments
- Struggled with addiction or mental health issues

If this describes your childhood experience, your own nervous system likely developed patterns designed to survive in that environment. You might find yourself:

- Hypervigilant for signs of danger or disapproval
- Quick to anger or defensiveness
- Prone to anxiety or panic responses
- Uncomfortable with intense emotions (your own or others')
- Struggling to stay present during your child's big feelings

Here's the hopeful truth: **your nervous system is neuroplastic, meaning it can continue to change and heal throughout your lifetime**. The same co-regulation process that helps your child can help you develop new patterns of regulation.

Working with a therapist, practicing mindfulness, building supportive relationships, and learning nervous system regulation skills can literally rewire your brain. As you develop greater capacity for staying present and calm during stress, you automatically offer your child a different template than the one you received.

Parent Self-Regulation Checklist

Developing awareness of your own nervous system states is the first step in becoming a co-regulating presence for your child. Use this checklist to assess your current regulation status:

Green Zone Indicators (Social Engagement Online):

- Face feels relaxed, natural expressions come easily

- Voice has normal rhythm and melody
- Breathing is slow and deep
- Body feels loose and comfortable
- Thoughts are clear and organized
- Able to make eye contact naturally
- Feel curious about your child's experience
- Can access empathy and compassion
- Able to problem-solve creatively

Yellow Zone Indicators (Sympathetic Activation Beginning):

- Slight tension in jaw, shoulders, or chest
- Breathing becoming shallower or faster
- Voice getting flatter or more controlled
- Starting to feel rushed or pressured
- Thoughts beginning to race or repeat
- Less able to see your child's perspective
- Urge to control or fix situations quickly
- Feeling mildly irritated or impatient

Red Zone Indicators (Full Fight-or-Flight):

- Heart rate noticeably increased
- Breathing rapid or held
- Muscles tense, especially face, jaw, neck
- Voice sharp, loud, or artificially calm
- Thoughts racing, worst-case scenarios

- Tunnel vision on problems or dangers

- Strong urge to argue, control, or escape

- Difficulty accessing empathy or humor

- Feeling overwhelmed, angry, or panicked

Blue Zone Indicators (Dorsal Shutdown):

- Feeling numb, disconnected, or empty

- Voice flat, monotone, or barely audible

- Body feels heavy or lifeless

- Thoughts slow, foggy, or blank

- Difficulty making eye contact

- Everything feels too hard or pointless

- Want to hide, sleep, or disappear

- Can't access caring or motivation

Regulation Thermometer for Family Members

Create a simple visual tool that helps your whole family recognize and communicate about nervous system states. You can draw this or create it digitally:

Green (Regulated): "I feel calm, happy, and ready to connect"
Yellow (Getting Activated): "I'm starting to feel stressed but can still think   clearly"
Orange (More Activated): "I'm feeling really stressed and need some help staying calm" **Red (Dysregulated):** "I'm overwhelmed and need space to calm down" **Blue (Shutdown):** "I'm feeling disconnected and need gentle help coming back"

Teach family members to check in with their own thermometer throughout the day and communicate their status to others. This creates a shared language for nervous system awareness and helps everyone respond to each other's states with understanding rather than judgment.

Breathing Exercises for Immediate Co-Regulation

When you notice your nervous system moving toward dysregulation, these breathing techniques can help you return to your social engagement system quickly:

4-7-8 Breathing (For Anxiety/Fight-or-Flight):

1. Exhale completely through your mouth

2. Inhale through your nose for 4 counts

3. Hold your breath for 7 counts

4. Exhale through your mouth for 8 counts

5. Repeat 3-4 times

This pattern activates your parasympathetic nervous system and signals safety to your brain.

Box Breathing (For General Stress):

1. Inhale for 4 counts

2. Hold for 4 counts

3. Exhale for 4 counts

4. Hold empty for 4 counts

5. Repeat 5-10 times

This creates a steady rhythm that helps regulate both your nervous system and your child's if they're nearby.

Belly Breathing with Your Child:

1. Sit or lie down together

2. Place one hand on chest, one on belly

3. Breathe so only the belly hand moves

4. Count together: "In, two, three, four... Out, two, three, four"

5. Make it playful: pretend to blow up balloons or smell flowers

This creates shared regulation through synchronized breathing and physical closeness.

Creating Your Family's Regulation Plan

A family regulation plan helps everyone know what to do when nervous systems get activated. Include these elements:

Early Warning System:

- How does each family member look/sound when getting dysregulated?

- What are the common triggers for each person?

- Who typically gets dysregulated first, and how does it spread?

Individual Regulation Strategies:

- What helps each family member return to calm?

- What makes dysregulation worse for each person?

- Where can family members go for space if needed?

Family Regulation Strategies:

- What can we do together to co-regulate?

- How do we handle it when multiple people are dysregulated?

- What's our repair process after everyone's calm?

Environmental Supports:

- How can we set up our home to support regulation?

- What changes do we need during stressful periods?

- When do we need to modify our expectations or routines?

Troubleshooting Guide When You're Both Dysregulated

It happens to every parent: your child is melting down, and instead of staying calm, you find yourself equally activated. Here's what to do:

If You're in Fight-or-Flight and Your Child Is Too:

1. **Create physical space immediately** - Move to different rooms if needed

2. **Focus on your own breathing first** - You can't co-regulate from dysregulation

3. **Use grounding techniques** - Feel your feet on the floor, notice five things you can see

4. **Wait for your voice to soften** before attempting to help your child

5. **Approach slowly with open body language** once you're calmer

If You're Shutting Down and Your Child Needs Support:

1. **Tell your child honestly: "I need a few minutes to feel better so I can help you"**

2. **Do something to increase your energy** - splash cold water, do jumping jacks, go outside

3. **Eat or drink something** if you haven't recently

4. **Call a friend or support person** if possible

5. **Start with small, simple interactions** rather than trying to solve the big problem

Emergency Regulation Strategies:

- **Humming or singing** (activates vagus nerve)

- **Cold water on wrists or face** (resets nervous system)

- **Progressive muscle relaxation** (tense and release muscle groups)

- **Call a regulated friend** for co-regulation support

- **Step outside** for fresh air and different environment

The key is accepting that you can't pour from an empty cup. Taking care of your own nervous system first isn't selfish—it's the prerequisite for being able to help your child.

The Long-Term Impact of Co-Regulation

When you consistently offer your child the experience of co-regulation—staying present and calm during their storms, helping their nervous system find its way back to safety—you're building their internal capacity for self-regulation.

Over time, children who experience reliable co-regulation develop:

- **Better emotional vocabulary** and self-awareness

- **Increased ability to calm themselves** when upset

- **Stronger relationships** based on trust and security

- **Greater resilience** in facing life's challenges

- **Improved physical health** due to better stress management

- **Enhanced learning capacity** because their brains aren't stuck in survival mode

Perhaps most importantly, they learn that relationships can be a source of healing and support rather than additional stress. This sets them up for healthy partnerships, parenting, and friendships throughout their lives.

Your nervous system truly is your child's GPS—constantly providing information about whether the world is safe or dangerous, whether relationships can be trusted, and how to navigate the ups and downs of being human. By developing your own capacity for regulation and understanding how your internal state affects your child, you give them the greatest gift possible: a nervous system that knows how to come home to safety.

Core Principles to Carry Forward:

- **Your nervous system state directly influences your child's regulation**

- **Co-regulation is more powerful than any parenting technique**

- **Children's brains are designed to sync with their caregivers**

- **You can heal your own nervous system patterns at any age**

- **Small moments of co-regulation create lasting change**

As we move into the next chapter, we'll explore how your child's unique temperament, sensitivities, and individual differences shape their specific window of tolerance and what this means for your co-regulation approach.

Chapter 3: Recognizing Your Child's Unique Window

Maria watched her twin boys play in the backyard, marveling at how different they could be despite sharing the same DNA, the same home, the same parents. Eight-year-old Carlos was building an elaborate fort with precise attention to detail, completely absorbed in his project. When a neighbor's dog started barking next door, he barely looked up.

Just ten feet away, his twin brother Diego had been happily kicking a soccer ball until that same dog started barking. Now Diego was covering his ears, his face scrunched up in distress, heading quickly toward the house. "The dog is too loud!" he called out, clearly overwhelmed by the noise that hadn't even registered with Carlos.

Same genetics. Same environment. Completely different windows of tolerance.

This scene plays out in families everywhere, and it can be both fascinating and frustrating for parents. Why does one child sail through situations that completely derail their sibling? Why do parenting strategies that work beautifully with one child seem to backfire with another? The answer lies in understanding that **every child comes into the world with their own unique nervous system blueprint**.

Your child's window of tolerance isn't just influenced by your parenting or their daily experiences—it's shaped by their individual temperament, sensory processing style, brain wiring, past experiences, and dozens of other factors that make them uniquely themselves.

Temperament and the Window

Temperament refers to the biologically-based individual differences in how children react to and interact with their environment (Thomas & Chess, 1977). Some children are born with naturally wider windows of tolerance, while others have more sensitive nervous systems that require extra support to stay regulated.

Understanding your child's temperamental style helps you work with their natural wiring rather than against it.

The Highly Sensitive Child

About 15-20% of children are born with a trait researchers call *high sensitivity* or *sensory processing sensitivity* (Aron, 2002). These children have nervous systems that process sensory information more deeply and thoroughly than average. Their windows of tolerance tend to be narrower, not because of weakness or deficiency, but because their brains are designed to notice more.

Characteristics of highly sensitive children:

- Notice subtle changes in environment (lighting, sounds, textures)
- Become overwhelmed more easily in stimulating situations
- Need more downtime to process experiences
- Show strong emotional reactions to movies, books, or conflicts
- Are deeply empathetic and concerned about others' feelings
- Prefer familiar routines and predictable environments
- May seem "shy" in new social situations
- Are often creative, thoughtful, and perceptive

How high sensitivity affects the window: Diego's reaction to the barking dog is typical for a highly sensitive child. His nervous system processes auditory input more intensely than his brother's. What feels like background noise to Carlos feels intrusive and overwhelming to Diego. This doesn't mean Diego is "weaker"—his brain is simply wired to be more aware of sensory information.

Highly sensitive children often have windows that narrow more quickly under stress and take longer to return to baseline. They benefit from:

- More preparation for new or stimulating situations

- Regular quiet time to decompress

- Validation that their sensitivity is a strength, not a problem

- Environmental modifications to reduce overwhelming input

- Extra time for transitions and processing

The Sensory-Seeking Child

On the other end of the spectrum are children whose nervous systems crave intense sensory input to feel regulated. These children often have naturally wide windows of tolerance and may actually become dysregulated when their environment is too calm or understimulating.

Characteristics of sensory-seeking children:

- Constantly moving, jumping, spinning, or crashing into things

- Seek out loud music, bright lights, or intense activities

- May seem "hyperactive" or have difficulty sitting still

- Love rough play and physical contact

- Often fearless in physical activities

- May not notice when they're hurt or uncomfortable

- Can handle chaotic environments better than peers

- Need high levels of stimulation to focus and learn

How sensory seeking affects the window: Carlos's ability to focus despite the barking dog reflects a nervous system that needs more intense input to feel activated. For sensory-seeking children, a quiet, calm environment might actually push them toward their red zone because their brains aren't getting enough stimulation to stay engaged.

These children benefit from:

- Structured opportunities for intense physical activity

- Fidget tools and movement breaks during focused activities

- Understanding that their need for stimulation isn't defiance

- Sensory-rich environments that feed their nervous systems

- Clear boundaries around safe vs. unsafe ways to get sensory input

Neurodivergent Windows

Children with neurodevelopmental differences like ADHD, autism, or learning disabilities often have unique window characteristics that require specialized understanding and support.

ADHD and Regulation

Children with ADHD have differences in executive function, attention regulation, and impulse control that directly impact their window of tolerance (Barkley, 2015). Their windows tend to be narrower and more variable, changing dramatically based on factors like interest level, time of day, and environmental demands.

ADHD characteristics affecting the window:

- Difficulty sustaining attention on non-preferred tasks

- Hyperfocus on highly interesting activities

- Impulsivity that increases when stressed or bored

- Emotional intensity and quick mood changes

- Sensitivity to criticism or perceived rejection

- Need for immediate feedback and reinforcement

- Executive function challenges that worsen under stress

Children with ADHD often experience *emotional dysregulation*—difficulty managing the intensity and duration of their emotional responses. Their windows can shift from green to red very quickly, and they may struggle to use traditional calming strategies effectively.

Autism and Sensory Windows

Autistic children often have unique sensory processing profiles that significantly impact their window of tolerance (Schaaf & Lane, 2015). They may be hypersensitive to certain inputs while seeking intense stimulation from others, creating complex regulation needs.

Autism characteristics affecting the window:

- Sensory sensitivities that vary by individual and situation

- Need for predictability and routine to maintain regulation

- Difficulty with transitions and unexpected changes

- Intense interests that can be both regulating and consuming

- Challenges with interoception (awareness of internal body signals)

- Different social communication styles that affect co-regulation

- Stimming behaviors that serve regulation functions

For autistic children, staying within their window often requires careful attention to sensory environments, predictable routines, and respect for their individual regulation strategies.

Cultural Factors in Emotional Expression and Regulation

Culture profoundly influences how children learn to express emotions and what regulation looks like in their family context (Matsumoto & Hwang, 2012). What appears to be dysregulation in one cultural context might be perfectly normal emotional expression in another.

Cultural variations in emotional expression:

- Some cultures encourage open emotional expression while others value emotional restraint

- Family communication styles affect how children learn to process and share feelings

- Religious or spiritual beliefs may influence how families understand emotional struggles

- Collectivist vs. individualist values impact approaches to independence and support-seeking

- Historical trauma in families or communities can affect nervous system patterns across generations

Implications for window awareness: A child from a family that values emotional expressiveness might have learned that big feelings are normal and acceptable, leading to a different window profile than a child from a family that emphasizes emotional control. Neither approach is right or wrong, but understanding your family's cultural context helps you interpret your child's regulation patterns accurately.

Consider how your own cultural background influences:

- What emotions feel comfortable for you to witness in your child

- How you respond to different types of emotional expression

- What regulation strategies feel familiar or foreign

- How you balance individual needs with family/community expectations

How Trauma Narrows the Window

Trauma—whether from a single overwhelming event or chronic stress—has a profound impact on children's nervous systems and significantly narrows their window of tolerance (van der Kolk, 2014). Children who have experienced trauma often live in a state of chronic hypervigilance, where their nervous systems are constantly scanning for danger.

Types of trauma affecting children:

- **Big T trauma:** Single overwhelming events like accidents, natural disasters, violence, or abuse

- **Little t trauma:** Chronic stressors like family conflict, poverty, discrimination, or emotional neglect

- **Medical trauma:** Painful or frightening medical procedures, chronic illness, or hospitalization

- **Developmental trauma:** Early disruptions in attachment relationships that affect brain development

How trauma affects the window: Trauma essentially reprograms the nervous system to prioritize survival over connection and learning. Children with trauma histories may:

- React intensely to triggers that seem minor to others

- Have difficulty trusting adult support during dysregulation

- Show delayed responses to stress (seeming fine initially, then melting down later)

- Struggle with sleep, appetite, or other basic regulation functions

- Display behaviors that seem controlling or manipulative but are actually survival strategies

- Have windows that vary dramatically based on trauma reminders in their environment

Supporting trauma-affected windows: Children with trauma histories need extra patience, predictability, and safety-building before their windows can begin to expand. Traditional parenting approaches that rely on consequences or time-outs can actually re-traumatize these children by triggering their abandonment fears.

Trauma-informed window support includes:

- Creating physical and emotional safety as the top priority

- Building trust slowly through consistent, caring responses

- Understanding that healing isn't linear—good days and bad days are both normal

- Working with trauma-informed therapists when needed

- Recognizing your own trauma responses and how they affect your child

The Role of Sleep, Nutrition, and Exercise

Basic biological needs have an enormous impact on every child's window of tolerance. A well-rested, well-fed child who gets regular physical activity has a much wider window than a child who is sleep-deprived, running on sugar, or sedentary.

Sleep and Regulation

Sleep is when the nervous system repairs and resets itself. Children who don't get adequate, quality sleep have significantly narrower windows of tolerance and recover more slowly from dysregulation (Meltzer & Mindell, 2014).

Sleep factors affecting the window:

- Total sleep duration (age-appropriate amounts)

- Sleep quality (deep, uninterrupted sleep cycles)

- Consistent sleep schedule (regular bedtimes and wake times)

- Sleep environment (dark, quiet, comfortable temperature)

- Screen exposure before bedtime (blue light disrupts melatonin)

A child who usually handles school stress well might fall apart over minor issues after a poor night's sleep. Their window hasn't permanently shrunk—it's temporarily narrowed due to insufficient nervous system recovery.

Nutrition and Blood Sugar

The brain runs on glucose, and unstable blood sugar levels directly impact emotional regulation. Children who go too long between meals, eat high-sugar foods without protein, or have food sensitivities may experience dramatic window fluctuations.

Nutritional factors affecting the window:
- Regular meal timing (preventing blood sugar crashes)

- Balanced meals with protein, complex carbs, and healthy fats

- Adequate hydration throughout the day

- Individual food sensitivities or allergies

- Micronutrient deficiencies (especially B vitamins, magnesium, omega-3s)

The classic "hangry" meltdown is a perfect example of how blood sugar affects the window. A child who seems unreasonably upset might simply need a healthy snack to return to regulation.

Movement and Nervous System Health

Physical activity is one of the most powerful regulation tools available. Exercise helps process stress hormones, builds resilience, and creates natural opportunities for nervous system reset (Ratey & Hagerman, 2008).

Movement factors affecting the window:

- Daily physical activity appropriate to child's age and abilities

- Variety of movement types (running, jumping, climbing, dancing)

- Outdoor time in nature when possible

- Opportunities for both structured and free play

- Regular movement breaks during sedentary activities

Children who seem chronically dysregulated often benefit dramatically from increasing their daily movement. This is especially true for sensory-seeking children whose nervous systems need physical input to stay organized.

Interoception and Body Awareness

Interoception is your child's ability to sense what's happening inside their body—hunger, thirst, heart rate, muscle tension, the need to use the bathroom, and emotional sensations (Craig, 2015). Strong interoceptive skills help children recognize when they're moving toward the edge of their window and take action before they become dysregulated.

Many children, especially those with neurodevelopmental differences or trauma histories, have weak interoceptive awareness. They might not notice they're hungry until they're having a meltdown, or they might not recognize building anxiety until they're in full panic mode.

Signs of weak interoception:

- Doesn't notice hunger, thirst, or need for bathroom until it's urgent

- Seems surprised by their own emotional reactions

- Difficulty describing how their body feels

- Doesn't recognize fatigue until they're exhausted

- Struggles to identify what helps them feel better

- May ignore or dismiss physical discomfort

Building interoceptive awareness:

- Regular body check-ins: "How does your stomach feel right now?"

- Teaching body part names and sensations

- Mindfulness activities that focus on physical sensations

- Movement activities that create strong body awareness

- Helping children connect body sensations to emotions

- Modeling your own interoceptive awareness out loud

Strong interoception essentially gives children an early warning system for their window of tolerance, allowing them to ask for help or use regulation strategies before they become overwhelmed.

Child Window Assessment Tool

To support your child's unique window, you first need to understand their individual patterns. This assessment tool helps you identify their specific characteristics:

Sensory Processing Style:

- How does your child respond to loud noises?

- Do they seek out or avoid intense sensory experiences?

- What types of touch are comforting vs. overwhelming?

- How do they handle busy, chaotic environments?

- What sensory inputs seem to calm them?

Emotional Intensity and Recovery:

- How quickly does your child move from calm to upset?

- How long do their emotional reactions typically last?
- What helps them return to calm most effectively?
- Do they internalize stress or express it outwardly?
- How do they handle disappointment or frustration?

Social and Environmental Factors:

- How does your child respond to new people or situations?
- Do they prefer predictable routines or enjoy surprises?
- How do they handle transitions between activities?
- What time of day is their window typically widest/narrowest?
- How does your mood/stress level affect their regulation?

Physical and Biological Factors:

- How does sleep quality affect their next-day regulation?
- Are there particular foods that seem to impact their behavior?
- How much daily movement do they need to stay regulated?
- Do they recognize their own body signals reliably?
- Are there medical factors that might affect their nervous system?

Daily Regulation Tracking Chart

Create a simple tracking system to identify your child's window patterns over time:

Morning Window Check:

- Sleep quality the night before (1-5 scale)
- Mood upon waking (green/yellow/red zone)
- Any obvious stressors or excitement for the day

- Physical complaints or energy level

Afternoon Assessment:

- How did morning activities go?
- Any regulation challenges or successes?
- Lunch/snack timing and content
- Energy and mood shifts

Evening Review:

- Overall window stability for the day
- What helped when dysregulation occurred?
- What triggered window exits?
- Preparation needed for tomorrow

Track for at least two weeks to identify patterns. You might notice that your child's window is consistently narrower on Mondays, or that certain activities predictably help or hinder their regulation.

Environmental Audit Checklist

Your child's physical environment significantly impacts their window of tolerance. Conduct an audit of spaces where your child spends time:

Home Environment:

- Is there a quiet space for decompression?
- Are sensory inputs (lighting, sound, clutter) at comfortable levels?
- Does your child have access to regulation tools when needed?
- Are daily routines and expectations clearly displayed?
- How does the energy level in your home typically feel?

School Environment:

- Does your child's teacher understand their regulation needs?

- Are there movement opportunities throughout the day?

- How is sensory input managed in the classroom?

- What support is available when your child becomes dysregulated?

- Are academic demands matched to your child's window capacity?

Social Environments:

- How do different social settings affect your child's regulation?

- Are there peers who seem to help or hinder their window?

- What social activities expand vs. contract their capacity?

- How can you prepare your child for challenging social situations?

Case Study: Maya, the Highly Sensitive Child

Eight-year-old Maya had always been described as "intense" and "dramatic" by well-meaning adults. She would come home from school completely overwhelmed, often melting down over seemingly minor issues like the wrong plate for dinner or a tag in her shirt feeling scratchy.

Her parents initially tried traditional approaches—consequences for the meltdowns, rewards for "good behavior," and encouragement to "toughen up." Nothing worked. Maya seemed to get more sensitive over time, not less.

Everything changed when Maya's parents learned about high sensitivity and began supporting her unique nervous system needs:

Environmental modifications: They created a calm-down corner in Maya's bedroom with soft lighting, weighted blankets, and noise-canceling headphones. After school, Maya spent 30 minutes in this space before any other activities.

Sensory preparation: Before potentially overwhelming situations, they would "prep" Maya's nervous system with deep pressure activities like tight hugs or rolling in a blanket.

Validation and education: Instead of dismissing Maya's sensitivity as overreaction, they helped her understand her nervous system and feel proud of her ability to notice details others missed.

Schedule adjustments: They built more downtime into Maya's schedule and became selective about after-school activities, choosing quality over quantity.

Within a few months, Maya's daily meltdowns decreased dramatically. She still had a sensitive nervous system, but she felt understood and supported rather than defective.

Case Study: Alex, the Intense/Spirited Child

Ten-year-old Alex was a force of nature. When happy, he was exuberantly joyful. When frustrated, his anger could fill the entire house. His emotions seemed to have only one volume: loud.

Alex's parents had tried everything—behavior charts, time-outs, taking away privileges—but his intense reactions continued. They felt like they were walking on eggshells, never knowing what might trigger his next explosion.

Understanding Alex's regulation patterns changed everything:

Emotional validation: Instead of trying to minimize Alex's big feelings, his parents learned to validate the intensity while setting boundaries around behavior: "You're really angry about this, and yelling at your sister isn't okay. Let's find a better way to handle these big feelings."

Preventive strategies: They identified Alex's early warning signs—rapid speech, increased movement, higher voice pitch—and intervened before he reached the red zone.

Physical outlets: Alex needed intense physical activity to process his big emotions. They created a "regulation station" in their garage with a punching bag, mini trampoline, and space to run around.

Processing time: After intense episodes, Alex needed time to decompress before any problem-solving or discussion could happen effectively.

Strengths focus: They helped Alex see his emotional intensity as a superpower that allowed him to feel joy, excitement, and passion more deeply than many people.

Alex still felt emotions intensely—that was part of his beautiful, spirited nature. But he learned to manage his big feelings in ways that didn't overwhelm his family or damage relationships.

Case Study: Jordan, the Anxious Child

Twelve-year-old Jordan had always been a worrier, but middle school seemed to trigger a new level of anxiety. She would lie awake at night catastrophizing about upcoming tests, friendship conflicts, or whether her parents were proud of her. Her window of tolerance had narrowed to the point where even minor stressors sent her into panic.

Jordan's parents initially tried reassurance and logical problem-solving, but these approaches seemed to make her anxiety worse. She would argue with their reassurances or find new things to worry about.

Supporting Jordan's anxious nervous system required a different approach:

Anxiety education: They taught Jordan about how anxiety works in the brain and body, helping her understand that anxious thoughts weren't facts but nervous system responses.

Body-based interventions: Instead of only addressing Jordan's worried thoughts, they focused on calming her physical symptoms through breathing exercises, progressive muscle relaxation, and movement.

Gradual exposure: Rather than avoiding anxiety triggers, they helped Jordan approach feared situations gradually, building confidence through small successes.

Routine and predictability: They established consistent routines that helped Jordan's nervous system feel safe and reduced daily uncertainty.

Professional support: They worked with a therapist who specialized in childhood anxiety to develop additional coping strategies.

Parent regulation: Jordan's parents learned to manage their own anxiety about her anxiety, recognizing that their worry was contributing to her dysregulation.

Jordan's anxiety didn't disappear overnight, but she developed tools to work with her nervous system rather than being controlled by it. Her window of tolerance gradually expanded as she felt more capable and supported.

Working with Your Child's Unique Blueprint

Every child's window of tolerance is as individual as their fingerprint. Your child's unique combination of temperament, sensory processing style, neurodevelopment, cultural background, life experiences, and biological factors creates a regulation profile that belongs only to them.

Understanding these individual differences allows you to:

- Set realistic expectations based on your child's actual capacity rather than comparison to peers

- Provide support that matches their nervous system needs rather than working against their wiring

- Celebrate their unique strengths while supporting their growing edges

- Advocate effectively for accommodations at school or in other settings

- Build their self-understanding and confidence in managing their own regulation

The goal isn't to make your child's window identical to someone else's. It's to help them understand their own nervous system, work with their natural patterns, and gradually expand their capacity in ways that feel sustainable and authentic.

Your child's differences aren't problems to be fixed—they're characteristics to be understood, supported, and celebrated. When you truly see your child's unique window of tolerance and respond to it with understanding rather than judgment, you give them the greatest gift possible: the experience of being fully accepted for who they are.

Fundamental Truths About Individual Differences:

- **Every child's nervous system is unique and deserves respect**

- **What works for one child may not work for their sibling**

- **Understanding differences prevents misinterpretation of behavior**

- **Support should match each child's individual needs and strengths**

- **Celebrating uniqueness builds confidence and self-awareness**

In the next chapters, we'll explore specific strategies for supporting different age groups, always keeping in mind that these approaches need to be tailored to your individual child's unique window of tolerance and nervous system characteristics.

Chapter 4: Toddler Storms

Co-Regulation in the Early Years (18 months-3 years)

Two-year-old Maya had turned bedtime into a nightly battleground. The moment her parents mentioned bath time, she would stiffen her body and start protesting. By the time they reached her bedroom, she was in full meltdown mode—screaming, throwing herself on the floor, and becoming increasingly inconsolable.

For months, her parents, Lisa and David, had tried everything they could think of. Strict bedtime routines, earlier or later bedtimes, rewards for cooperation, consequences for resistance. Nothing worked. If anything, Maya's bedtime storms were getting worse.

Then Lisa learned about window of tolerance and toddler brain development. She realized they had been asking Maya's nervous system to do something it literally couldn't do—self-regulate under stress. That night, everything changed.

Instead of rushing through the bedtime routine while Maya escalated, Lisa slowed down. When Maya started getting tense during bath time, Lisa sat on the bathroom floor and took some deep breaths. "I can see your body is getting worried about bedtime. Let me help you feel safe."

She offered Maya a choice between two pajama options, sang a familiar song while Maya brushed her teeth, and created a cozy nest of blankets on the floor next to Maya's bed. "Your nervous system needs help settling down. Mama's going to stay right here until you feel calm."

Instead of the usual hour-long battle, Maya was asleep within twenty minutes. Not because she had suddenly learned self-control, but because her nervous system finally felt supported rather than overwhelmed.

Why Toddler Brains Can't Self-Regulate

If you've ever felt frustrated by your toddler's inability to "just calm down" when upset, you're not alone. But here's what's actually happening in their developing brain: **the neural circuits responsible for self-regulation don't come online until around age four, and they're not fully mature until the mid-twenties** (Zelazo et al., 2003).

Your toddler's prefrontal cortex—the brain region responsible for executive functions like impulse control, emotional regulation, and logical thinking—is barely developed. It's like expecting someone to drive a car when they only have access to the gas pedal and not the brakes.

What toddlers do have:

- A fully functioning limbic system (emotional brain) that detects threats and activates survival responses

- Mirror neurons that sync their nervous system with yours

- An attachment system designed to seek co-regulation from caregivers

- Rapidly developing neural pathways that are shaped by repeated experiences

What toddlers don't have:

- Ability to calm themselves down when dysregulated

- Understanding of time concepts like "in five minutes" or "after lunch"

- Capacity to use logic during emotional storms

- Skills to communicate complex needs and feelings verbally

- Impulse control when wanting something immediately

This isn't a character flaw or parenting failure—it's normal brain development. Your toddler's dramatic reactions aren't manipulation; they're neurobiological responses from a nervous system that's completely dependent on your co-regulation.

The prefrontal cortex develops gradually through childhood and adolescence, with different executive function skills coming online at different times. Working memory begins developing around age 3-4, cognitive flexibility around age 4-5, and inhibitory control continues developing well into the teenage years (Diamond, 2013). This means your toddler is operating almost entirely from their emotional brain, with minimal input from their thinking brain.

The Narrowest Windows

Toddlers have the narrowest windows of tolerance of any age group. Their capacity for handling stress, stimulation, and emotional intensity is extremely limited, and their recovery time is longer than older children's.

Factors that make toddler windows especially narrow:

- **Immature nervous system:** Their stress response system is hypersensitive and slow to return to baseline

- **Limited communication skills:** They can't express complex needs, leading to frustration and dysregulation

- **Rapid development:** Their brains are changing so quickly that their regulation capacity varies day by day

- **Dependency needs:** They require constant co-regulation from adults but can't ask for it directly

- **Sensory overwhelm:** Their filtering systems aren't developed, so they notice everything equally

A toddler's window might be wide enough to handle getting dressed *or* eating breakfast *or* saying goodbye to a parent, but not all three in succession. What looks like a child "falling apart over nothing" is usually a nervous system that has reached its daily capacity.

Understanding toddler nervous system capacity: Think of your toddler's nervous system like a small battery that drains quickly and takes a long time to recharge. Every demand—physical, emotional, or cognitive—uses battery power. A well-rested toddler might start the day with a full battery, but by afternoon, even small requests can trigger big reactions because their system is depleted.

The Build-Up, Storm, and Recovery Pattern

Toddler emotional storms follow predictable patterns once you understand their nervous system responses:

The Build-Up Phase:

- Increased movement or restlessness

- Changes in voice tone or volume

- Difficulty following simple directions

- Seeking more physical contact or pushing away

- Minor frustrations leading to bigger reactions

The Storm Phase:

- Full activation of fight-or-flight response

- Crying, screaming, or aggressive behaviors

- Physical symptoms like flushed face, rapid breathing

- Inability to hear or process language

- Complete overwhelm of their system

The Recovery Phase:

- Gradual decrease in intensity
- Physical exhaustion from the stress response
- Need for comfort, connection, and co-regulation
- Return to baseline can take 20-40 minutes
- Often followed by clingy or regressive behaviors

Many parents try to intervene during the storm phase, but this is when your toddler's thinking brain is completely offline. The most effective interventions happen during the build-up phase or focus on supporting recovery.

Tantrums vs. Meltdowns

Not all toddler emotional storms are the same. Understanding the difference between tantrums and meltdowns helps you respond appropriately to what your child's nervous system actually needs.

Tantrums (Goal-Directed Behavior):

- Child wants something specific and is using big emotions to get it
- May escalate when they get attention but stop when ignored
- Child maintains some awareness of their surroundings
- Behaviors may be somewhat controlled or strategic
- Child can often be distracted or redirected
- Usually shorter in duration (5-15 minutes)

Meltdowns (Nervous System Overwhelm):

- Child is completely overwhelmed and cannot control their response

- Getting bigger reactions indicates genuine distress

- Child has no awareness of surroundings or consequences

- Behaviors are completely involuntary

- Child cannot be reasoned with, distracted, or redirected

- Often longer in duration (20-60 minutes) with extended recovery time

Why this distinction matters: Tantrums might respond to boundary-setting and not giving in to demands, but meltdowns require co-regulation and nervous system support. Trying to set boundaries during a meltdown can actually make it worse because you're asking a dysregulated nervous system to access skills it doesn't currently have.

Most toddler emotional storms are actually meltdowns—nervous system overwhelm rather than manipulative behavior. When in doubt, respond with co-regulation first. If it's truly a tantrum, providing calm support won't reinforce the behavior. If it's a meltdown, punishment or ignoring can actually traumatize a child whose system is already overwhelmed.

Building Secure Attachment Through Co-Regulation

Every time you help your toddler move from dysregulation back to calm, you're building their attachment security and laying the foundation for their future self-regulation skills (Bowlby, 1988).

The co-regulation process with toddlers:

1. **You stay calm** when they become dysregulated

2. **You move physically closer** (if they'll allow it) to offer your regulated presence

3. **You validate their experience** without trying to fix or minimize it

4. **You offer comfort** through your voice, touch, or presence

5. **You wait** for their nervous system to settle before problem-solving

6. **You reconnect** once they're back in their window of tolerance

This process teaches your toddler that:

- Big feelings are manageable and temporary
- Relationships are a source of safety and support
- Adults can be trusted to help during difficult moments
- Their nervous system can return to calm after activation
- They are worthy of love even when they're struggling

Secure attachment markers in toddlers:

- Seeks comfort from caregivers when distressed
- Can be soothed relatively quickly with support
- Explores environment confidently when feeling safe
- Shows preference for familiar caregivers but can warm up to others
- Recovers from separation and reunites warmly
- Generally cooperative when their needs are met

The co-regulation process literally shapes your toddler's developing brain architecture. When you consistently respond to their distress with calm presence and support, you're building neural pathways that will serve them throughout their lives.

Language Development and Emotional Vocabulary

Toddlers are just beginning to develop language skills, and emotional vocabulary comes later than basic communication. Most toddlers can't accurately identify or express their internal states, which contributes to their dysregulation.

Typical emotional language development:

- **18-24 months:** Basic feeling words like "mad," "sad," "happy"

- **2-2.5 years:** Beginning to connect feelings to situations ("Mad! No nap!")

- **2.5-3 years:** More complex emotional expressions ("I scared of the dog")

- **3+ years:** Starting to understand emotional nuance and multiple feelings

Supporting emotional vocabulary development:

- **Label emotions for them:** "You're feeling frustrated that the block tower fell down"

- **Use simple, concrete language:** "Mad feelings" instead of "frustrated"

- **Connect emotions to body sensations:** "Your mad feelings made your hands tight"

- **Validate all feelings:** "It's okay to feel scared. Mama's here."

- **Read books about emotions** and point out feeling faces

- **Model emotional language:** "I feel excited about going to the park!"

Don't expect toddlers to use emotional vocabulary independently yet—you're building the foundation for skills they'll develop later. When you consistently label their emotions for them, you're helping them develop the neural connections between their internal experiences and language.

Routine as Regulation

Predictable routines are like nervous system medicine for toddlers. When they know what's coming next, their stress response system can relax instead of constantly scanning for potential threats or changes.

Why routines support toddler regulation:

- **Reduce uncertainty** which triggers stress responses
- **Build executive function** through repeated sequences
- **Create safety** through predictability
- **Support transitions** between activities
- **Establish circadian rhythms** for sleep and eating
- **Provide structure** that feels containing rather than controlling

Effective toddler routines include:

- **Visual cues** like pictures showing the sequence of activities
- **Consistent timing** for meals, naps, and bedtime
- **Transition warnings** like "five more minutes of blocks"
- **Built-in regulation breaks** between stimulating activities

- **Flexibility** for days when windows are narrower than usual

- **Connection moments** woven throughout the day

A routine isn't a rigid schedule—it's a predictable flow that supports your toddler's developing nervous system. The goal is creating enough structure to provide safety while maintaining enough flexibility to respond to your child's changing needs.

The PEACE Method for Toddler Meltdowns

When your toddler is in full meltdown mode, this five-step approach helps you provide effective co-regulation:

P - Pause and Breathe Before you do anything else, take three deep breaths. Your nervous system state is the most powerful tool you have for helping your toddler regulate. If you're activated, you can't co-regulate effectively. This pause also prevents you from reacting from your own stress response.

E - Empathize and Validate
Acknowledge your toddler's experience without trying to fix it: "You're having such big feelings right now. This is really hard for you." Don't try to talk them out of their feelings or minimize their experience. Validation helps them feel understood and supported.

A - Attune to Their Needs Try to understand what their nervous system needs in this moment. Do they need space? Comfort? Sensory input? Connection? Trust your instincts about what might help. Sometimes they need you close, sometimes they need you nearby but not touching.

C - Connect Before You Correct Focus on reestablishing emotional connection before addressing any behavior. This might mean sitting quietly nearby, offering a hug, or just staying present until they're ready. Don't try to teach lessons or set boundaries while they're dysregulated.

E - Evaluate and Learn After everyone is calm, reflect on what might have triggered the meltdown and what helped during recovery. This information helps you support your toddler's regulation more effectively next time. Look for patterns in timing, triggers, and effective interventions.

Sensory Soothing Toolkit for Ages 1-3

Toddlers often need specific sensory input to help their nervous systems regulate. Having a toolkit of sensory strategies helps you support them quickly during dysregulation.

Calming Sensory Strategies:

- **Deep pressure:** Bear hugs, weighted lap pad, or rolling in a blanket

- **Rhythmic movement:** Rocking, swaying, or gentle bouncing

- **Soft textures:** Favorite stuffed animal, soft blanket, or fuzzy pillow

- **Quiet sounds:** Humming, soft singing, or white noise

- **Dim lighting:** Turning down lights or closing curtains

- **Familiar scents:** Lavender lotion or a piece of parent's clothing

Alerting Sensory Strategies (for low energy/shutdown):

- **Cold input:** Cool washcloth on face or ice cube to suck on

- **Upbeat music** or silly songs

- **Crunchy snacks** like crackers or apples

- **Bright lights** or going outside

- **Movement activities** like jumping or dancing

- **Strong tastes** like lemon or peppermint

Heavy Work Activities (organizing for the nervous system):

- **Pushing or pulling** heavy objects like a laundry basket

- **Carrying** books, toys, or other weighted items

- **Wall pushes** or "helping" move furniture

- **Playing with playdough** or other resistive materials

- **Animal walks** like bear crawls or crab walks

- **Squeezing** stress balls or stuffed animals

The key is having multiple options available because what works one day might not work the next, and different types of dysregulation need different sensory approaches.

Transition Strategies That Prevent Dysregulation

Transitions are particularly challenging for toddlers because they require flexible thinking and tolerance for uncertainty—skills their brains haven't developed yet. Most toddler meltdowns happen during transitions, so preventing them is often more effective than managing them.

Why transitions are hard for toddlers:

- **Difficulty with time concepts:** Can't understand "in five minutes"

- **Attachment to current activity:** Leaving something fun feels like loss

- **Uncertainty about what's next:** Unknown situations trigger stress responses

- **Executive function demands:** Transitions require mental flexibility they don't possess yet

- **Sensory adjustments:** Moving between environments with different sensory demands

Effective transition strategies:

- **Give advance warning:** "In five minutes, we're going to clean up the toys"

- **Use visual cues:** Timer, pictures, or songs to signal transitions

- **Create transition rituals:** Special song, countdown, or routine that bridges activities

- **Offer choices:** "Do you want to hop like a bunny or walk like a robot to the car?"

- **Bring comfort objects:** Favorite toy or blanket to ease the transition

- **Stay calm yourself:** Your regulation during transitions teaches them that changes are manageable

Common transition challenges:

- **Leaving fun activities:** Build in extra time and use countdown warnings

- **Morning routines:** Create visual schedules and prepare the night before

- **Bedtime:** Start wind-down activities early and use consistent routines

- **Daycare drop-off:** Develop goodbye rituals and transition objects

- **Getting dressed:** Offer choices and make it playful rather than rushed

The key is making transitions predictable and giving toddlers' nervous systems time to adjust to change rather than demanding immediate compliance.

Time-In vs. Time-Out

Traditional time-outs ask dysregulated toddlers to calm down in isolation, which goes against everything we know about co-regulation and attachment. Time-ins offer a connection-based alternative that actually builds regulation skills.

Why time-outs don't work for toddlers:

- **Isolation triggers attachment fears** in developing brains

- **Asks for self-regulation skills** they don't possess yet

- **Can increase stress** rather than supporting recovery

- **Misses opportunity** for co-regulation and learning

- **May work temporarily** but doesn't build long-term skills

- **Can damage the parent-child relationship** by using disconnection as punishment

Time-in approach:

- **Stay physically close** during your child's big emotions

- **Offer comfort and co-regulation** rather than isolation

- **Wait for calm** before discussing behavior or problem-solving

- **Maintain connection** even when setting boundaries

- **Focus on safety** and nervous system support first

What time-in looks like:

- Sitting nearby while your toddler has their feelings

- Offering gentle touch if they want it (not forcing physical comfort)

- Using a calm, soothing voice to narrate what's happening

- Waiting for their storm to pass before addressing behavior

- Reconnecting with warmth once they're regulated

Time-in doesn't mean permissiveness—you still maintain boundaries and safety. But you do it in a way that supports rather than overwhelms their developing nervous system.

Visual Schedules and First-Then Boards

Toddlers understand pictures before they fully understand language. Visual supports help them know what to expect and feel more in control of their environment, which supports their window of tolerance.

Visual schedule benefits:

- **Reduce anxiety** about what's coming next

- **Support memory** for multi-step routines

- **Increase independence** in following routines

- **Provide predictability** that supports regulation

- **Help with transitions** between activities

Creating effective visual schedules:

- **Use real photos** of your child doing activities when possible

- **Keep it simple** with 3-5 pictures maximum for toddlers

- **Place at child's eye level** where they can easily see it

- **Review together** at the beginning of routines

- **Let child move or remove pictures** as activities are completed

First-then boards help with immediate transitions:

- "First we clean up toys, then we have snack"

- "First we put on shoes, then we go outside"

- Use two pictures showing the sequence clearly

- Particularly helpful for non-preferred activities followed by preferred ones

Visual supports work because they give toddlers a sense of predictability and control, which expands their window of tolerance and makes cooperation more likely.

Age-Specific Tools for Toddler Regulation

Emotion Faces Chart for Toddlers

Create a simple chart with 4-6 basic emotion faces that you can reference throughout the day:

Essential emotions for toddlers:

- **Happy:** Big smile, bright eyes

- **Mad:** Frowning mouth, angry eyebrows

- **Sad:** Tears, downturned mouth

- **Scared:** Wide eyes, worried expression

- **Tired:** Droopy eyes, yawning mouth

- **Excited:** Wide smile, raised eyebrows

Use real photos of your toddler making these faces if possible. Point to the chart during daily activities: "Look, you have a mad face just like this picture!" This helps them begin to connect internal feelings with external expressions.

Calming Corner Setup Guide

Create a special space in your home where your toddler can go for regulation support:

Essential elements:

- **Soft seating:** Bean bag, floor cushions, or soft blanket
- **Comfort items:** Favorite stuffed animals or soft toys
- **Sensory tools:** Stress ball, fidget toys, or textured items
- **Books about feelings:** Simple picture books about emotions
- **Music or sound machine:** Soft, calming sounds
- **Dim lighting:** Table lamp or string lights rather than overhead lighting

Important guidelines:

- Make it inviting, not punitive—this isn't a place for time-outs
- Let your toddler help choose items for the space
- Use it yourself to model self-regulation
- Keep it easily accessible but not in high-traffic areas
- Change items occasionally to maintain interest

Toddler Breathing Games

Make breathing exercises playful and engaging for little ones:

Bubble Breathing:

- Pretend to blow bubbles slowly and gently

- Inhale to "dip the bubble wand," exhale to "blow the bubble"

- Count bubbles together: "One bubble... two bubbles..."

- Use real bubbles occasionally to make it concrete

Flower Breathing:

- "Smell the flower" (slow inhale through nose)

- "Blow out the candle" (slow exhale through mouth)

- Use real flowers when possible for sensory engagement

- Make different flower "smells" for variety

Teddy Bear Breathing:

- Lie down with stuffed animal on belly

- Watch teddy "ride the waves" as belly goes up and down

- Make it a cozy, connecting activity rather than a task

- Let your toddler choose which stuffed animal to use

Heavy Work Activities List

These activities help organize the nervous system when toddlers are dysregulated:

Indoor activities:

- **Push walking:** Walking while pushing a sturdy chair or toy across the floor

- **Carrying jobs:** Moving books, toys, or laundry baskets

- **Wall pushes:** "Help me move this wall" - push against wall for 10 seconds

- **Pillow sandwich:** Squeeze child gently between couch cushions

- **Dance party:** Jumping, stomping, and moving to music
- **Playdough play:** Squeezing, rolling, and manipulating resistive materials

Outdoor activities:

- **Playground equipment:** Swings, slides, and climbing structures
- **Sandbox digging:** Using hands or tools to dig in sand
- **Water play:** Carrying watering cans or pushing/pulling water toys
- **Chalk drawing:** Drawing on sidewalks with large chalk pieces
- **Nature collecting:** Filling containers with rocks, leaves, or sticks
- **Walking/hiking:** Physical movement in natural settings

The key is offering these activities when you notice your toddler getting dysregulated, not waiting until they're already in full meltdown mode.

Building Long-Term Regulation Skills

Maya's bedtime transformation didn't happen overnight. Lisa and David learned to:

Recognize Maya's early warning signs - tensed shoulders, higher voice, increased resistance to instructions

Adjust expectations based on her daily window - easier bedtimes after low-key days, extra support after stimulating activities

Build regulation breaks into their routine - quiet time after bath, dimmed lights during story time, snuggles before bed

Stay regulated themselves - taking deep breaths, moving slowly, speaking softly even when Maya was escalating

Celebrate small improvements - shorter recovery times, asking for help instead of melting down, using feeling words

Most importantly, they learned that Maya's big emotions weren't a reflection of their parenting failure. They were normal responses from a developing nervous system that needed co-regulation support.

Three months later, bedtime had transformed from a battleground into a connecting ritual. Maya still had challenging days and difficult emotions—she was still a toddler, after all. But her parents now had tools to support her developing nervous system rather than fight against it.

Core Principles for Toddler Co-Regulation:

- **Your calm presence is more powerful than any technique**

- **Connection must come before correction or teaching**

- **Big emotions are normal and necessary for healthy development**

- **Co-regulation builds the foundation for future self-regulation**

- **Every storm weathered together strengthens your relationship**

The toddler years can be exhausting and overwhelming, but they're also a precious window when you're literally building your child's capacity for lifelong emotional health. Your patience, understanding, and regulatory support during these early storms creates the neural pathways your child will rely on for decades to come.

The foundation you build during the toddler years—through consistent co-regulation, emotional validation, and nervous system support—becomes the launching pad for all future regulation development. The toddler who experienced their big feelings as manageable with support becomes the preschooler who can recognize their internal states, the school-age child who can ask for help when overwhelmed, and the teenager who trusts relationships as sources of support during difficult times.

Chapter 5: Preschool Foundations

Teaching Self-Awareness (Ages 3-5)

Four-year-old Marcus stood in his preschool classroom, his small hands balled into fists, his face flushed red. His teacher, Ms. Sarah, had just announced that they needed to clean up the blocks and transition to circle time. But Marcus wasn't ready. He'd been building the most amazing castle, and now everyone wanted him to destroy it.

"I don't want to!" he yelled, his voice getting higher and louder. "My castle isn't finished!"

Six months ago, this scene would have escalated quickly. Marcus would have thrown blocks, screamed until he couldn't catch his breath, and spent the next hour in dysregulated misery. His teachers would have used time-outs, consequences, and frustrated redirections that only made things worse.

But everything changed when Marcus's parents and teachers learned about his developing nervous system. That day in the classroom, instead of demanding immediate compliance, Ms. Sarah knelt down to Marcus's eye level and spoke calmly.

"I can see your body has fast feelings about stopping your castle work. Your hands look tight and your face looks hot. Let's help your body slow down first."

She placed her hand gently on her own chest and took a visible, deep breath. "My body is going to help your body remember how to feel slow and calm."

Marcus watched his teacher's face, noticed her relaxed shoulders, heard her quiet voice. Something in his nervous system started to settle. After a minute, Ms. Sarah continued.

"Your castle is really special to you. I can see why you want to keep building. What if we take a picture of it so you can keep working on it later? And maybe we can ask the other kids to help us carefully move it to the shelf so it stays safe."

Instead of the usual meltdown, Marcus took a shaky breath and nodded. His nervous system was learning something crucial: adults could help him recognize his internal states and support him through difficult transitions.

This is what the preschool years are all about—children developing the building blocks of self-awareness while still needing tremendous co-regulation support.

Emerging Self-Regulation Capabilities

The preschool years mark a fascinating transition in children's nervous system development. While toddlers operate almost entirely from their limbic system (emotional brain), preschoolers are beginning to develop the neural connections that will eventually support self-regulation (Zelazo et al., 2003).

What's developing in the preschool brain:

- **Early executive function skills:** Beginning ability to stop, think, and make different choices
- **Emotional vocabulary:** Can name basic feelings and sometimes connect them to situations
- **Theory of mind:** Starting to understand that other people have different thoughts and feelings
- **Working memory:** Can hold simple instructions in mind for short periods
- **Cognitive flexibility:** Beginning ability to switch between different activities or rules
- **Inhibitory control:** Developing capacity to stop impulses (though still very limited)

What's still developing:

- **Prefrontal cortex maturation:** The thinking brain won't be fully online until the mid-twenties

- **Stress recovery:** Takes much longer to return to baseline after dysregulation than adults

- **Complex problem-solving:** Can't think through multi-step solutions independently

- **Emotional regulation:** Still needs significant co-regulation support during big feelings

- **Impulse control:** Physical impulses often override verbal instructions

This means preschoolers live in a fascinating in-between space. They're no longer completely dependent on co-regulation like toddlers, but they can't yet manage their emotions independently. They're developing self-awareness but still need tremendous support to use that awareness effectively.

Introduction to Body Speeds and Zones

One of the most helpful concepts for preschoolers is learning to recognize their internal states through simple, concrete language. The idea of "body speeds" helps children begin to develop interoceptive awareness—the ability to notice what's happening inside their body.

Body Speed Concepts for Preschoolers:

Slow Body (Blue Zone):

- Feels tired, sleepy, or sad

- Hard to pay attention or move around

- Might want to hide or be alone

- Voice is quiet or whisperey

- Needs help waking up their body

Just Right Body (Green Zone):

- Feels calm, happy, and ready to learn
- Can listen to instructions and follow rules
- Plays nicely with friends
- Voice is normal volume
- Body feels good and comfortable

Fast Body (Yellow Zone):

- Feels excited, silly, or worried
- Hard to sit still or focus
- Might talk really fast or loud
- Starting to feel overwhelmed
- Needs help slowing down

Super Fast Body (Red Zone):

- Feels angry, scared, or totally overwhelmed
- Can't think clearly or make good choices
- Might yell, hit, or run away
- Body feels out of control
- Needs lots of help calming down

Teaching body speeds effectively:

- Use consistent language across all settings (home, school, with all caregivers)
- Connect body speeds to physical sensations kids can notice

- Practice identifying body speeds during calm moments, not just crises

- Help children see that all body speeds are normal and temporary

- Teach strategies that match each body speed rather than expecting one-size-fits-all solutions

Play as Regulation Practice

Play is how preschoolers naturally practice regulation skills. Through play, they experiment with different emotions, practice impulse control, negotiate with peers, and learn to recover from disappointment—all while having fun (Gray, 2013).

Types of regulation practice through play:

Imaginative Play:

- Playing "house" or "school" lets children practice managing different emotions safely

- Role-playing helps them understand other perspectives and develop empathy

- Creating stories allows them to work through fears and anxieties

- Taking on different characters helps them experiment with self-control

Physical Play:

- Running, jumping, and climbing help regulate their nervous systems

- Games with rules teach impulse control and frustration tolerance

- Rough-and-tumble play (when appropriate) helps with body awareness

- Dancing and movement activities provide natural emotional release

Creative Play:

- Art, music, and building activities offer calming regulation opportunities
- Creative expression helps process emotions that can't be verbalized yet
- Sensory play (playdough, sand, water) provides nervous system organization
- Cooperative creating teaches turn-taking and flexibility

Social Play:

- Playing with peers provides natural opportunities to practice co-regulation
- Sharing and taking turns require impulse control and emotional flexibility
- Conflicts during play offer real-time regulation practice with adult support
- Group games teach children to stay regulated even when excited or disappointed

Supporting regulation through play:

- Follow your child's lead rather than controlling their play
- Offer co-regulation support during play conflicts without taking over
- Use play themes to address regulation challenges ("The teddy bear is having big feelings too")
- Build regulation breaks into play sessions before children become overstimulated

- Celebrate moments when children self-regulate during play

Peer Interactions and Co-Regulation Challenges

Preschoolers are just beginning to learn how to be in relationships with peers, and this creates unique regulation challenges. Unlike the predictable co-regulation they receive from familiar adults, peer interactions are unpredictable and emotionally intense.

Common peer-related regulation challenges:

- **Sharing and taking turns:** Requires impulse control that's still developing

- **Different play styles:** Some children need high stimulation while others get overwhelmed easily

- **Emotional contagion:** One child's dysregulation quickly spreads to others

- **Social conflicts:** Disagreements can escalate rapidly without adult support

- **Exclusion or rejection:** Triggers deep attachment fears in young children

- **Competition:** Can overwhelm developing nervous systems

Supporting peer regulation:

- **Teach empathy concretely:** "Look at Sam's face. How do you think his body is feeling?"

- **Practice social scripts:** Give children actual words to use in common situations

- **Build in regulation breaks:** Don't expect sustained peer interaction without breaks

- **Support rather than solve:** Help children work through conflicts rather than fixing everything

- **Model peer co-regulation:** Show children how to help friends feel better

- **Create structured opportunities:** Organized activities are easier than completely free play

Signs your preschooler needs peer interaction support:

- Consistently aggressive or withdrawn with other children

- Cannot play cooperatively for more than a few minutes

- Becomes dysregulated every time they're around peers

- Shows intense emotional reactions to minor peer conflicts

- Avoids or fears social situations with other children

School Readiness Through Window Awareness

Traditional "school readiness" focuses on academic skills—knowing letters, numbers, and colors. But true school readiness is actually regulation readiness—the ability to stay calm enough to learn in a group setting (Blair & Diamond, 2008).

Regulation-based school readiness skills:

- **Can separate from parents** without prolonged distress

- **Follows simple routines** with minimal adult support

- **Asks for help** when feeling overwhelmed rather than melting down

- **Recovers from disappointments** relatively quickly with support

- **Plays cooperatively** with peers for reasonable periods

- **Transitions between activities** without major resistance

- **Sits and attends** for age-appropriate periods (3-5 minutes per year of age)

- **Communicates basic needs** including bathroom, hunger, and discomfort

Building school readiness at home:

- **Practice group activities:** Library story time, playground visits, family gatherings

- **Establish predictable routines:** Morning sequences that mirror school structure

- **Build attention span gradually:** Start with 5-minute focused activities and slowly increase

- **Practice following instructions:** Simple, one-step directions that build success

- **Develop independence skills:** Self-care tasks that build confidence

- **Create social opportunities:** Playdates that provide peer practice with support

Working with preschool teachers: Share information about your child's unique window of tolerance, including:

- What helps them stay regulated during transitions

- Early warning signs when they're becoming overwhelmed

- Effective calming strategies for their nervous system

- Any triggers or sensitivities teachers should know about

- How long they typically need to recover from dysregulation

Managing Separation Anxiety

Separation anxiety is normal and healthy in preschoolers—it shows that they have strong attachments. But when children's windows of tolerance are narrow, separation can trigger intense nervous system responses that interfere with their ability to engage in preschool activities.

Why preschoolers experience separation anxiety:

- **Developing sense of time:** They can't understand "Mommy will pick you up after snack"

- **Attachment system activation:** Their nervous system interprets separation as potential danger

- **Limited coping skills:** They don't yet have independent regulation strategies

- **Big developmental leaps:** Starting school represents huge change and uncertainty

- **Individual temperament:** Sensitive children may have stronger separation responses

Supporting healthy separation:

- **Start gradually:** Brief separations with familiar caregivers before longer preschool days

- **Create connection rituals:** Special handshakes, drawings, or comfort objects that maintain connection

- **Use transitional objects:** Something that smells like home or represents family connection

- **Build relationships with teachers:** When children trust their teachers, separation feels safer

- **Validate feelings while maintaining boundaries:** "You're sad that Daddy left, and he'll be back after outdoor play"

- **Avoid sneaking away:** This breaks trust and increases anxiety about future separations

When separation anxiety needs extra support:

- Child cannot be comforted by teachers after 30-60 minutes

- Intense reactions continue after several weeks of consistent routine

- Child refuses to eat, use bathroom, or participate in any activities

- Physical symptoms like headaches or stomachaches appear

- Child becomes aggressive or withdrawn in response to separation

The Zones of Regulation Adapted for Preschoolers

The Zones of Regulation, developed by Leah Kuypers, provides a framework that works beautifully for preschoolers when adapted to their developmental level. The four colored zones help children begin to categorize their internal states and learn appropriate responses.

Preschooler-Friendly Zone Descriptions:

Blue Zone (Slow Body):

- "My body feels slow, tired, or sad"

- "I might want to be quiet or rest"

- "My energy is low like a turtle"

- Tools: Energizing activities, movement, upbeat music, snacks

Green Zone (Just Right Body):

- "My body feels calm and ready to learn"

- "I can follow directions and play with friends"

- "My energy is just right like a steady tree"

- Tools: Continue current activities, maintain routine

Yellow Zone (Getting Fast):

- "My body is getting excited, worried, or wiggly"

- "I'm starting to feel overwhelmed but can still think"

- "My energy is getting high like a bouncing ball"

- Tools: Deep breaths, movement breaks, fidget toys, quiet activities

Red Zone (Too Fast):

- "My body feels out of control"

- "I can't think clearly or make good choices"

- "My energy is too high like a tornado"

- Tools: Adult support, calming strategies, safe space, time to recover

Teaching zones effectively:

- Use colors, pictures, and simple language consistently

- Practice identifying zones during calm moments

- Connect zones to body sensations ("butterflies in your tummy means yellow zone")

- Help children notice triggers that move them between zones

- Teach zone-appropriate tools rather than expecting one strategy to work for everything

Storytelling for Emotional Literacy

Preschoolers are natural storytellers, and stories provide a powerful way to help them understand emotions and regulation. Through stories, children can safely explore big feelings and practice coping strategies without real-world consequences.

Types of regulation stories:

Personal Stories:

- Tell stories about your child's successful regulation: "Once there was a little boy who felt really angry when his tower fell down. But then he took some deep breaths and asked for help building it even taller..."

- Include challenges and solutions: Show the process of moving from dysregulation to regulation

- Make your child the hero: They solved the problem with support and tools

Therapeutic Stories:

- Create stories that address specific challenges your child faces

- Use animal characters or other children rather than making it obviously about your child

- Include multiple solutions so children can choose what resonates with them

- End with the character feeling proud and capable

Book Selection:

- Choose books that show characters experiencing and managing big emotions

- Look for stories where adults provide support rather than punishment

- Avoid books where problems are solved through magic or external fixes

- Select books that validate emotions while showing healthy coping

Interactive Storytelling:

- Let children add details or change story elements

- Ask "What do you think the character is feeling?" questions

79

- Practice the coping strategies the story characters use

- Encourage children to tell their own regulation stories

Movement Breaks and Regulation Stations

Preschoolers need movement to regulate their nervous systems. Extended periods of sitting or quiet activities often lead to dysregulation because their bodies need sensory input to stay organized.

Creating effective movement breaks:

- **Every 15-20 minutes:** Brief movement opportunities during focused activities

- **Scheduled gross motor time:** Daily outdoor play or indoor physical activities

- **Transition movements:** Use movement to help shift between activities smoothly

- **Individual movement needs:** Some children need more, others need calmer movement

- **Environmental considerations:** Safe spaces both indoors and outdoors

Regulation station ideas:

Calming Station:

- Soft cushions, weighted lap pads, noise-canceling headphones

- Books, quiet music, dim lighting

- Stress balls, fidget toys, textured materials

- Art supplies for quiet creative work

Alerting Station:

- Crunchy snacks, cold water, peppermint scents

- Bright lights, upbeat music
- Movement tools like mini trampolines or balance boards
- Games that require focus and attention

Heavy Work Station:

- Resistance bands, therapy balls, weighted objects to carry
- Play dough, therapy putty, stress balls to squeeze
- Push/pull activities like moving chairs or books
- Deep pressure activities like being sandwiched between cushions

Teaching children to use regulation stations:

- Practice during calm times so they know how to access tools when needed
- Help them identify which tools work best for different feelings
- Allow autonomous use while providing gentle guidance
- Celebrate when children recognize their needs and seek appropriate support

Building Frustration Tolerance Through Supported Challenges

Preschoolers need to experience manageable frustration to build resilience, but the key word is "manageable." Challenges need to be just difficult enough to stretch their skills without overwhelming their developing nervous systems.

Principles of supported challenge:

- **Start within their window:** Begin with tasks they can accomplish with minimal support
- **Gradually increase difficulty:** Add small challenges as their confidence builds

81

- **Provide scaffolding:** Offer just enough support to prevent complete overwhelm
- **Celebrate effort over outcome:** Focus on trying rather than succeeding perfectly
- **Allow natural consequences:** Let them experience mild frustration while staying nearby for support

Examples of appropriate challenges:

- **Puzzles:** Start with 6-8 pieces, gradually increase complexity
- **Building projects:** Simple structures they can complete independently with minimal help
- **Self-care tasks:** Dressing, brushing teeth, simple food preparation
- **Social challenges:** Sharing, taking turns, working through minor conflicts
- **Creative projects:** Art or craft activities with some challenging steps

Supporting children through frustration:

- Stay calm and present when they struggle
- Validate their feelings: "This is hard work! Your brain is getting stronger."
- Offer specific encouragement: "I saw you try three different ways to make that piece fit"
- Help them break big tasks into smaller steps
- Teach simple coping strategies: deep breaths, asking for help, taking breaks

Preschool-Specific Resources and Tools

Feeling Thermometer Craft Activity

Create a visual tool that helps preschoolers identify their emotional intensity:

Materials needed:

- Large poster board or cardboard
- Red, yellow, and green construction paper
- Markers, crayons, or colored pencils
- Laminator or clear contact paper (optional)
- Velcro or magnetic strips

Instructions:

1. Draw a large thermometer shape on the poster board
2. Divide it into sections: green (bottom), yellow (middle), red (top)
3. Let your child decorate each section and add feeling faces
4. Create moveable arrows or markers to show current feeling level
5. Practice using it during different emotional states throughout the day

How to use:

- Check in with the thermometer several times daily during calm moments
- Help your child identify where their feelings are on the thermometer
- Discuss what tools or strategies work for each level
- Use it to communicate with teachers or other caregivers about your child's needs

Social Stories for Common Triggers

Create simple stories that help your preschooler navigate challenging situations:

Format for social stories:

- Use simple, concrete language
- Include pictures or drawings when possible
- Focus on what your child CAN do, not just what they shouldn't do
- Keep them short (3-5 sentences)
- Practice reading them regularly, not just during crises

Sample social story for transitions: "Sometimes at preschool, my teacher says it's time to clean up. When I hear 'clean up time,' my body might feel fast or worried. That's okay. I can take a deep breath and ask my teacher for help. When I clean up my toys, I feel proud of my helpful hands."

Common trigger topics:

- Leaving fun activities
- Sharing toys with friends
- Using the bathroom at school
- Sitting for circle time
- Trying new foods at snack time
- Handling disappointment when things don't go as planned

Calm-Down Cards with Pictures

Create a deck of visual cards showing regulation strategies:

Card ideas:

- Deep breathing (show child breathing slowly)

- Counting to ten (show fingers counting)
- Asking for help (child talking to adult)
- Using fidget toys (hands squeezing stress ball)
- Taking space (child in cozy corner)
- Drinking water (child with water bottle)

How to use:

- Keep cards in easily accessible locations
- Practice using them during calm times
- Let your child choose which cards to try
- Add new cards as your child learns new strategies
- Share copies with teachers for consistent support

Parent-Teacher Collaboration Template

Information to share with teachers:

My Child's Unique Window:

- Typical daily regulation patterns (best/worst times of day)
- Individual triggers that narrow their window
- Early warning signs of dysregulation
- Effective calming strategies
- How long they typically need to recover

Communication Preferences:

- How often to receive updates about regulation challenges
- Whether you want to know about minor incidents or only major ones
- Best ways to reach you during the school day

- Information you'd like shared with substitutes or specialists

Support Strategies:

- Specific accommodations that help your child succeed

- Sensory tools or comfort objects that are helpful

- Language that works well for your child

- Connection with home routines that could be reinforced at school

Goals We're Working On:

- Current regulation skills your child is developing

- Areas where they need extra support

- Celebrations and progress you want to acknowledge together

Looking Ahead - Building on Preschool Foundations

The preschool years lay crucial groundwork for your child's lifelong relationship with their emotions and nervous system. During this time, you're helping them develop:

- **Self-awareness:** The ability to notice their internal states

- **Emotional vocabulary:** Words to describe their experiences

- **Coping strategies:** Tools that actually work for their unique nervous system

- **Relationship skills:** Trust that adults can help during difficult moments

- **Resilience:** Confidence that they can handle challenges with support

Marcus's journey shows how this process unfolds. Six months after learning about body speeds and zones, he had developed remarkable self-awareness for a four-year-old. When his teacher announced cleanup time, he might still feel disappointed about stopping his play. But now he could say, "My body feels fast because I don't want to stop building."

His teacher could respond with understanding rather than control: "Thank you for telling me about your fast body. What would help your body feel slower so we can clean up together?"

This shift—from demanding compliance to supporting regulation—transforms the entire preschool experience. Children learn to see adults as allies rather than opponents. They develop confidence in their ability to handle big feelings. Most importantly, they begin to understand their own nervous systems and trust that they have tools to help themselves.

Essential Foundations for Preschool Success:

- **Body awareness leads to emotional awareness**

- **Play is the natural laboratory for practicing regulation skills**

- **Peer interactions require significant adult support at this age**

- **School readiness is regulation readiness more than academic readiness**

- **Challenges should stretch skills without overwhelming the nervous system**

As we transition into the school-age years, these preschool foundations become the launching pad for more sophisticated regulation strategies and greater independence. The child who learned to recognize their "fast feelings" at age four is well-prepared to handle academic stress and peer pressure at age eight.

The investment you make in supporting your preschooler's nervous system development pays dividends for decades to come.

Chapter 6: School-Age Strategies

Expanding Windows in a Wider World (Ages 6-11)

Nine-year-old Aisha sat at her desk, staring at the math test in front of her. Her heart was beating so fast she could hear it in her ears. The numbers on the page seemed to swim around, and her mind went completely blank. This was her worst subject, and she knew her parents were expecting a good grade.

Her hands started to shake. Her breathing got shallow and quick. The familiar panic was setting in—the same feeling that had been happening every time she faced a test lately.

But then Aisha did something different. Instead of letting the panic take over, she placed one hand on her chest and one on her belly, just like her mom had taught her. She took three slow, deep breaths and whispered to herself, "My nervous system is just trying to protect me. I can handle this feeling."

She noticed her body sensations—the tight shoulders, the clenched jaw, the butterflies in her stomach. "Yellow zone," she thought. "Getting activated but still able to think."

Aisha had learned that she could acknowledge her anxiety without being controlled by it. She used a technique her family called "body wisdom meets brain power"—honoring what her nervous system was telling her while using her developing cognitive skills to respond thoughtfully.

She looked at the first problem again. Still difficult, but now she could actually see the numbers clearly. She might not get every answer right, but she could handle whatever came up. Her window of tolerance had expanded enough to hold both the challenge of the test and her natural anxiety about it.

This is what the school-age years are all about—children developing increasingly sophisticated ways to understand and work with their nervous systems while navigating a much more complex world.

Academic Stress and the Window of Tolerance

School-age children face unprecedented demands on their developing nervous systems. Unlike preschoolers who spend most of their time in play-based activities, elementary-age children must sustain attention, follow complex instructions, manage peer relationships, and perform academically—all while their prefrontal cortex is still years away from maturity.

The modern school environment often creates a perfect storm for narrow windows of tolerance (Immordino-Yang & Damasio, 2007). Children are expected to sit still for extended periods, process large amounts of information, compete with peers, and manage multiple subjects and teachers throughout the day.

Academic stressors that narrow children's windows:

- **Performance pressure:** Tests, grades, and comparisons with other students

- **Sustained attention demands:** Sitting still and focusing for increasingly long periods

- **Complex instructions:** Multi-step directions that tax working memory

- **Social-academic combination:** Learning while managing peer dynamics and teacher relationships

- **Time pressure:** Rushed schedules with little downtime between demanding activities

- **Overstimulating environments:** Noisy classrooms, bright fluorescent lights, crowded spaces

Signs your school-age child's window is narrowing due to academic stress:

- Sunday night anxiety or Monday morning meltdowns

- Physical complaints (headaches, stomachaches) that increase during school days

- Resistance to homework that seems disproportionate to the task

- Sleep difficulties or nightmares about school

- Regression in behaviors (bedwetting, clinginess, baby talk)

- Emotional outbursts immediately after school

- Perfectionist tendencies or complete avoidance of challenging tasks

Supporting your child's academic window: The key is helping your child develop both **body awareness** and **cognitive strategies** to manage academic demands. Aisha's success with her test anxiety came from combining nervous system regulation (breathing, body awareness) with cognitive tools (self-talk, problem-solving).

This integration of somatic and cognitive approaches becomes possible during the school-age years as children's abstract thinking abilities develop while they still maintain strong connections to their bodily experiences.

Peer Pressure and Social Regulation

The social world becomes exponentially more complex during the school-age years. Children are managing friendships, group dynamics, social hierarchies, and peer expectations while their social brains are still developing (Steinberg, 2013).

Social challenges that impact regulation:

- **Friendship complexity:** Learning to navigate conflicting loyalties and changing alliances

- **Social comparison:** Constant comparison with peers in academics, athletics, appearance, and popularity

- **Group dynamics:** Inclusion/exclusion patterns that trigger deep attachment fears

- **Social rules:** Unspoken rules about what's "cool" or acceptable that change frequently

- **Identity formation:** Figuring out who they are in relation to their peer group

- **Bullying or social conflict:** Dealing with meanness, exclusion, or aggression from peers

How peer stress affects the nervous system: Social rejection activates the same brain areas as physical pain (Eisenberger, 2012). For school-age children who are developmentally focused on peer acceptance, social stress can be as dysregulating as physical danger.

Children might maintain perfect regulation at school to fit in socially, then completely fall apart at home where they feel safe to release all that stored stress. The child who seems fine all day but has massive meltdowns every afternoon may be using tremendous energy to stay regulated in social situations.

Building social regulation skills:

- **Teach emotional granularity:** Help children identify specific social emotions (embarrassed, excluded, proud, envious) rather than just "good" or "bad"

- **Practice perspective-taking:** "What do you think Sarah was feeling when that happened?"

- **Develop social problem-solving:** Role-play common social scenarios and practice multiple response options

- **Build confidence in authentic self-expression:** Help children understand they don't need to change themselves to be accepted by real friends

- **Create social safety at home:** Make home a place where they can process social stress without judgment

Building Interoception and Body Awareness

Interoception—the ability to sense internal bodily signals—becomes increasingly important during the school-age years as children face more complex emotional and social situations. Strong interoceptive skills help children recognize when their window of tolerance is narrowing and take action before they become completely dysregulated.

Research shows that children with better interoceptive awareness have improved emotional regulation, decision-making, and social relationships (Garfinkel et al., 2015). Yet many school-age children, especially those with neurodivergent nervous systems, struggle to recognize their internal states until they're already overwhelmed.

Interoceptive signals school-age children can learn to notice:

- **Heart rate changes:** Racing heart during anxiety, slow heart rate when tired

- **Breathing patterns:** Shallow breathing when stressed, deep breathing when calm

- **Muscle tension:** Tight shoulders when worried, clenched jaw when frustrated

- **Temperature changes:** Feeling hot when angry, cold when scared or sad

- **Digestive sensations:** Butterflies when nervous, nausea when overwhelmed, hunger affecting mood

- **Energy levels:** Feeling wired when overstimulated, sluggish when understimulated

Activities to build interoceptive awareness:

Body Scanning: Teach children to do quick "body check-ins" throughout the day:

- "Start at the top of your head and notice how each part of your body feels"

- "What do you notice in your chest? Your stomach? Your hands?"

- "Is any part of your body holding tension or feeling different than usual?"

Movement and Body Awareness:

- **Yoga or stretching:** Activities that require attention to body positioning and sensation

- **Dancing:** Free movement that helps children notice how different emotions feel in their body

- **Sports and physical activities:** Natural opportunities to notice heart rate, breathing, muscle fatigue

- **Heavy work activities:** Carrying, pushing, or pulling that provides strong proprioceptive input

Mindful Activities:

- **Eating meditation:** Noticing taste, texture, hunger, and fullness cues

- **Nature observation:** Sitting quietly outside and noticing both environmental and internal sensations

- **Art and creativity:** Activities that engage both body and mind simultaneously

Homework Battles Through a Regulation Lens

Homework conflicts are rarely about the actual academic content—they're usually about nervous system states and mismatched expectations. When you understand homework battles as regulation challenges, everything changes.

Why homework triggers dysregulation:

- **Depleted window:** After a full day of school demands, children's regulation capacity is often exhausted

- **Transition challenges:** Moving from play/relaxation mode back to academic focus

- **Performance anxiety:** Fear of making mistakes or disappointing parents

- **Executive function demands:** Homework requires planning, organization, and sustained attention when these skills are tired

- **Parent stress contagion:** When parents feel anxious about homework completion, children absorb that stress

The regulation-first approach to homework:

Step 1: Assess the window before starting

- How was your child's day? High stress, normal, or particularly good?

- What's their current nervous system state? Do they need to release energy, calm down, or wake up their system?

- Are they hungry, thirsty, or need to use the bathroom?

- What kind of support does their nervous system need before engaging their thinking brain?

Step 2: Match the environment to their needs

- Some children need quiet, low-stimulation environments to focus

- Others need background music, fidget tools, or movement opportunities
- Consider lighting, seating options, and proximity to you
- Remove distractions that overwhelm their filtering systems

Step 3: Start with connection

- Spend a few minutes connecting before jumping into homework
- Ask about their day, share something about yours
- Use humor, physical affection, or other ways of ensuring they feel emotionally safe with you

Step 4: Break tasks into window-appropriate chunks

- Match the difficulty and length of tasks to your child's current capacity
- Build in regulation breaks between subjects or challenging problems
- Celebrate effort and problem-solving, not just correct answers

Step 5: Stay regulated yourself

- Your nervous system state directly impacts theirs
- If you feel yourself getting frustrated, take a break
- Focus on connection and effort rather than perfect completion

Sports, Competition, and Emotional Regulation

Athletic activities provide tremendous opportunities for school-age children to practice regulation skills, but they can also create intense stress that narrows windows of tolerance. The key is helping children develop healthy relationships with competition and performance.

Benefits of sports for regulation:

- **Physical outlet:** Natural way to process stress hormones and regulate the nervous system

- **Embodied learning:** Direct experience with effort, resilience, and recovery

- **Team co-regulation:** Learning to stay calm when teammates are stressed

- **Goal-setting practice:** Working toward improvements over time rather than seeking perfection

- **Emotional intensity:** Safe environment to experience and manage strong feelings

Sports-related regulation challenges:

- **Performance pressure:** From coaches, parents, or self-imposed expectations

- **Social dynamics:** Team conflicts, playing time issues, or competitive peer relationships

- **Physical intensity:** High arousal that can tip into anxiety or anger

- **Win/lose emotions:** Managing disappointment, frustration, or overwhelming excitement

- **Comparison with others:** Measuring self-worth through athletic performance

Supporting athletic regulation:

- **Focus on effort over outcome:** Celebrate trying hard, learning new skills, and team cooperation

- **Teach pre-performance regulation:** Breathing exercises, visualization, or physical warm-ups that calm the nervous system

- **Process emotions after games:** Help children identify and express feelings about their performance

- **Model healthy competition:** Show them how to compete intensely while maintaining respect for opponents

- **Balance intensity with recovery:** Ensure adequate rest, nutrition, and non-competitive physical activities

Technology's Impact on the Nervous System

Modern school-age children navigate technology use in ways that can significantly impact their nervous system regulation. Screen time isn't inherently good or bad, but it does affect developing brains in specific ways that parents need to understand.

How technology affects nervous system regulation:

Dopamine and Reward Circuits:

- Gaming, social media, and video content trigger dopamine release in unpredictable patterns

- This can make other activities (homework, chores, face-to-face conversation) feel boring by comparison

- Children may need increasingly stimulating content to feel engaged

Sleep and Circadian Rhythms:

- Blue light exposure, especially in evening, disrupts melatonin production

- Stimulating content before bed makes it harder for the nervous system to wind down

- Poor sleep quality narrows windows of tolerance the following day

Attention and Focus:

- Rapid content changes train brains to expect constant stimulation

- Extended focus on single tasks becomes more challenging

- Children may struggle with boredom tolerance and need external entertainment

Social Connection:

- Online interactions can supplement but not replace face-to-face social regulation

- Social media can trigger comparison and FOMO (fear of missing out) that increase anxiety

- Reduced face-to-face time may impact development of social regulation skills

Creating healthy technology boundaries:

- **Use regulation before and after screens:** Help children notice their nervous system state before technology use and support their transition back to off-screen activities

- **Balance stimulating and calming content:** Include educational, creative, or calming screen activities alongside entertainment

- **Create tech-free connection time:** Regular periods for face-to-face interaction and co-regulation

- **Model healthy relationships with technology:** Let children see you managing your own screen time mindfully

- **Teach body awareness during technology use:** Help children notice how different types of screen time affect their energy, mood, and sleep

Cognitive Strategies Meet Somatic Awareness

The school-age years offer a unique opportunity to help children integrate their developing cognitive abilities with body awareness. This combination creates more robust regulation skills than either approach alone.

Cognitive developments that support regulation:

- **Abstract thinking:** Can understand concepts like "nervous system" and "window of tolerance"

- **Future thinking:** Can anticipate challenging situations and prepare strategies

- **Self-reflection:** Beginning ability to notice their own thought and behavior patterns

- **Problem-solving:** Can generate multiple solutions to emotional and social challenges

- **Metacognition:** Thinking about thinking—awareness of their own mental processes

Somatic awareness that remains strong:

- **Body-based emotions:** Still feel emotions primarily in their bodies before thinking about them

- **Sensory sensitivity:** Notice environmental factors that affect their regulation

- **Movement needs:** Require physical activity to maintain optimal nervous system functioning

- **Intuitive responses:** Often have "gut feelings" about people and situations that are accurate

Integrating cognitive and somatic approaches:

Thinking AND Feeling Strategies:

- "What is my body telling me about this situation, and what does my thinking brain say?"

- "I notice my heart is racing (body awareness) and I'm thinking that everyone will judge me (cognitive awareness)"

- "My stomach feels tight, which usually means I'm worried about something. Let me think about what might be bothering me."

Problem-Solving with Body Wisdom:

- "What does my body need right now to help my brain work better?"

- "When I tried that solution, how did it feel in my body? Did it actually help or just seem like it should help?"

- "Let me try this strategy and notice what happens in both my thoughts and my physical sensations."

Peer Conflict Resolution Skills

School-age children need concrete skills for handling the increasingly complex social conflicts they encounter. These skills need to account for how stress affects their nervous systems and provide tools that work when emotions are high.

The CALM method for peer conflicts:

C - Check your nervous system

- "How is my body feeling right now?"

- "Am I in my green zone and able to think clearly?"

- "Do I need to take some deep breaths or get adult help before trying to solve this?"

A - Acknowledge both perspectives

- "I can see that you're upset about this too"

- "We both want different things right now"

- "This situation is hard for both of us"

L - Listen to understand, not to win

- "Help me understand what happened from your point of view"

- "What would make this situation feel better for you?"

- "Is there something I did that hurt your feelings?"

M - Make a plan together

- "What could we try that might work for both of us?"

- "How can we prevent this from happening again?"

- "Should we ask a grown-up to help us figure this out?"

Teaching conflict resolution effectively:

- Practice during calm moments, not in the middle of actual conflicts

- Role-play common scenarios with family members

- Help children identify their personal conflict triggers

- Teach them when to seek adult support rather than handling everything independently

- Celebrate successful conflict resolution, even when the solution isn't perfect

Study Environment Optimization

School-age children benefit from learning environments that support their individual nervous system needs. There's no one-size-fits-all study environment, but there are principles that help most children focus and learn effectively.

Environmental factors that affect regulation and learning:

Sensory Environment:

- **Lighting:** Natural light is ideal; avoid harsh fluorescent lights when possible

- **Sound:** Some children need quiet while others focus better with background music or white noise

- **Visual distractions:** Clear, organized spaces help children with attentional challenges

- **Seating options:** Some children focus better standing, sitting on exercise balls, or in alternative seating

- **Temperature:** Room temperature that's comfortable for sustained focus

Organizational Systems:

- **Clear materials organization:** Everything has a designated place and is easily accessible

- **Visual schedules:** Charts showing homework routine or assignment due dates

- **Time management tools:** Timers, calendars, or apps that help with planning and pacing

- **Break spaces:** Designated areas for regulation breaks during homework time

Creating individualized study environments:

- Observe when and where your child naturally focuses best

- Experiment with different environmental modifications

- Ask your child what helps them concentrate and what's distracting

- Adjust the environment based on their current nervous system state

- Be willing to change setups as your child grows and their needs shift

After-School Decompression Routines

The transition from school to home is often the most dysregulated time of day for school-age children. They've been managing their nervous systems in a demanding environment for 6-8 hours, and they often release all that stored stress the moment they feel safe at home.

Why after-school meltdowns happen:

- **Accumulated stress:** Small stressors throughout the day add up to overwhelm by afternoon

- **Masking exhaustion:** Children work hard to appear regulated at school, then collapse at home

- **Transition challenges:** Shifting from structured school environment to less structured home environment

- **Hunger and low blood sugar:** Often haven't eaten adequately during busy school day

- **Social processing:** Need time to process complex peer interactions and social situations

Creating effective decompression routines:

Immediate Needs (First 15-30 minutes):

- **Physical comfort:** Comfortable clothes, bathroom break, physical affection if wanted

- **Nutrition:** Healthy snack that stabilizes blood sugar

- **Sensory reset:** Whatever their nervous system needs most—movement, quiet time, or sensory input

- **Emotional safety:** No demands for academic performance or detailed day reports

Processing Time (30-60 minutes):

- **Unstructured play:** Time to engage in activities they choose

- **Physical activity:** Running, jumping, dancing, or other movement to discharge stress

- **Creative expression:** Art, music, or imaginative play that doesn't require performance

- **Social connection:** Time with family members without academic pressure

Gradual Re-Engagement:

- **Transition activities:** Bridge between decompression and evening responsibilities

- **Collaborative planning:** Involve child in deciding homework timing and approach

- **Connection before direction:** Ensure emotional connection before giving instructions or expectations

Building Emotional Vocabulary and Nuance

School-age children's expanding language abilities allow them to develop much more sophisticated emotional vocabulary. This expanded emotional literacy directly supports regulation by helping children identify and communicate their internal states more precisely.

Moving beyond basic emotions: Instead of just "mad, sad, glad, scared," school-age children can learn to identify:

Anger family: frustrated, irritated, furious, annoyed, outraged, indignant **Sadness family:** disappointed, discouraged, heartbroken, melancholy, grieving, lonely **Fear family:** worried, nervous, anxious, terrified, startled, overwhelmed **Joy family:** content, excited, proud, grateful, cheerful, enthusiastic **Complex emotions:** embarrassed, jealous, guilty, ashamed, confused, relieved

Teaching emotional nuance:

- **Read books** that explore complex emotions and discuss characters' feelings

- **Share your own emotional experiences** using specific vocabulary

- **Help children notice** the difference between similar emotions (frustrated vs. furious)

- **Connect emotions to body sensations** ("Embarrassed feels hot in your face, while nervous feels fluttery in your stomach")

- **Validate all emotions** while teaching appropriate expression

School-Age Tools and Resources

Homework Regulation Plan

Create a personalized plan that accounts for your child's nervous system needs:

Daily Routine Assessment:

- What time does your child typically arrive home?

- How much decompression time do they need before homework?

- What does their nervous system usually need after school (movement, quiet, food, connection)?

- When is their optimal homework time based on energy and focus patterns?

Environmental Setup:

- Where does your child focus best?

- What sensory supports help them concentrate?

- How can you minimize distractions during homework time?

- What materials and organizational systems do they need?

Regulation Supports:

- What are your child's early warning signs of homework stress?

- Which regulation strategies work best for them during academic tasks?

- How long can they typically focus before needing a break?

- What helps them transition between subjects or tasks?

Family Approach:

- How will you stay regulated during homework time?

- What's your plan when homework becomes a conflict?

- How will you balance support with building independence?

- What will you do if homework consistently triggers dysregulation?

Test Anxiety Toolkit

Help your child develop specific strategies for managing test-related stress:

Before the Test:

- **Preparation strategies** that build confidence without creating pressure

- **Sleep and nutrition** guidelines for test days

- **Morning routines** that support regulation

- **Positive self-talk** scripts they can use

During the Test:

- **Breathing techniques** that can be used discretely in class

- **Body awareness** strategies to notice and address tension

- **Cognitive strategies** for managing racing thoughts or blanking out
- **Problem-solving approaches** when they encounter difficult questions

After the Test:

- **Processing feelings** about their performance
- **Learning from the experience** without harsh self-judgment
- **Celebrating effort** regardless of outcomes
- **Planning improvements** for future tests

Weekly Family Regulation Meetings

Institute regular family meetings focused on nervous system awareness and regulation:

Meeting Structure (15-20 minutes):

- **Check-ins:** Each family member shares their regulation highlights and challenges from the week
- **Problem-solving:** Work together on regulation challenges anyone is facing
- **Planning ahead:** Anticipate stressful situations and plan regulation support
- **Celebration:** Acknowledge growth in regulation skills and family support

Topics to Address:

- Individual regulation patterns and needs
- Environmental changes that would support family regulation
- Stressful upcoming events and how to prepare for them
- Regulation successes and lessons learned

- Family rules or routines that need adjustment

Making meetings effective:

- Keep them brief and positive

- Focus on solutions rather than criticism

- Include everyone's perspective, including younger children

- Make them collaborative rather than parent-directed

- End with connection activities or family appreciation

The Growing Window

Marcus, the preschooler we met in the previous chapter who learned about "fast feelings," is now seven years old. His regulation skills have expanded dramatically, but not in the way his parents initially expected.

He still feels emotions intensely—that's part of his temperament and always will be. But now he has language for his experiences and tools that actually work for his nervous system. When he feels overwhelmed by homework, he can say, "My brain feels scrambled and my body feels tight. I think I need to bounce on my exercise ball for five minutes before I try this math again."

His parents learned to see his emotional intensity as information rather than a problem to fix. They worked with his nervous system rather than against it, and built his capacity gradually over time.

This is what the school-age years offer—not the elimination of big feelings or challenges, but the development of increasingly sophisticated ways to understand and work with their unique nervous systems. Children like Aisha learn that they can feel anxious AND handle tests. They can experience peer conflict AND use skills to resolve it. They can feel overwhelmed by homework AND ask for the support they need.

Building Blocks for School-Age Success:

- **Academic demands require both cognitive and somatic regulation strategies**

- **Peer relationships become increasingly central to nervous system regulation**

- **Interoceptive awareness provides early warning systems for dysregulation**

- **Technology use significantly impacts developing nervous systems**

- **After-school decompression is essential for most school-age children**

- **Emotional vocabulary expansion supports more precise regulation**

The school-age window of tolerance expands not because children learn to suppress their emotions or needs, but because they develop better tools for understanding and working with their internal experiences. They learn that their nervous systems are sources of valuable information, not obstacles to overcome.

As we move into the teenage years, these school-age foundations become the launching pad for navigating even more complex emotional, social, and developmental challenges. The nine-year-old who learned to breathe through test anxiety is well-prepared to handle the identity challenges and social pressures of adolescence.

Chapter 7: Teen Transitions

Navigating the Adolescent Nervous System (Ages 12-18)

Jordan scrolled through Instagram at 2 AM, heart racing as they compared their life to the highlight reels flooding their screen. What started as a quick check for messages had turned into a three-hour spiral of social comparison, leaving them feeling anxious, inadequate, and wide awake when they desperately needed sleep for tomorrow's chemistry test. Sound familiar? This scenario plays out in millions of homes every night, but Jordan's story has a different ending than most.

When Jordan's mom, Lisa, discovered her teenager still awake at 2:30 AM, she didn't launch into a lecture about screen time or responsibility. Instead, she recognized the signs of nervous system dysregulation and gently helped Jordan navigate back to their window of tolerance. "I can see your system is really activated right now," she said softly, sitting on the edge of the bed. "Let's help your nervous system settle so you can actually get some rest."

Within twenty minutes, Jordan was breathing steadily, phone charging in another room, and drifting off to sleep. The difference? Lisa understood that her teenager's brain was undergoing the most dramatic reconstruction since infancy, and traditional parenting approaches often miss this crucial reality.

The adolescent years bring unique challenges to the window of tolerance framework. Unlike younger children who rely primarily on external co-regulation, teenagers are learning to self-regulate while their brains undergo massive changes. This creates a perfect storm of narrowed windows, intense emotions, and desperate needs for both connection and independence.

Understanding the teenage nervous system isn't just helpful—it's essential for maintaining your relationship and supporting your adolescent's healthy development. When we approach teen behaviors through the lens of nervous system awareness rather than defiance or disrespect, everything changes.

The Adolescent Brain Revolution

The teenage brain is essentially under construction for a decade. From ages 12 to 25, your adolescent's neural architecture is being completely remodeled. This isn't a gentle renovation—it's more like demolishing walls while trying to live in the house.

The prefrontal cortex, responsible for executive functions like decision-making, impulse control, and emotional regulation, is the last part of the brain to mature. Meanwhile, the limbic system, which processes emotions and rewards, is hypersensitive during these years. This creates what neuroscientist Dr. Frances Jensen calls "all gas, no brakes" (Jensen, 2015).

Research from Temple University shows that the mere presence of peers can increase risk-taking behavior in teenagers by up to 50%, even when those peers aren't encouraging risky choices (Chein, Albert, O'Brien, Uckert, & Steinberg, 2011). This isn't about rebellion—it's about biology.

The window of tolerance naturally narrows during adolescence because of this neural remodeling. What looked like emotional stability in your 11-year-old might suddenly seem to disappear at 13. This temporary narrowing is normal and expected, but it catches many parents off guard.

Think of your teenager's brain like a city undergoing major infrastructure updates. The roads are torn up, detours are everywhere, and getting from point A to point B takes much longer than usual. Your teen isn't choosing to be more emotional or impulsive—they're working with a brain that's literally under construction.

Dr. Laurence Steinberg's research demonstrates that while cognitive abilities reach adult levels by age 16, the brain systems responsible for self-control don't fully mature until the mid-twenties (Steinberg,

2013). This explains why your teenager can write a brilliant essay about the dangers of texting and driving, then text while driving the next day.

Puberty's Impact on Emotional Regulation

Puberty doesn't just change bodies—it revolutionizes the nervous system. Hormonal fluctuations affect neurotransmitter function, sleep patterns, and stress responses. Estrogen and testosterone don't just influence physical development; they directly impact emotional reactivity and stress sensitivity.

Research shows that cortisol levels, our primary stress hormone, increase significantly during puberty (Romeo, 2010). This means teenagers are physiologically more reactive to stress than children or adults. What might be a minor frustration for an adult can feel overwhelming to a teenager's hypersensitive nervous system.

Sleep patterns shift dramatically during adolescence due to changes in melatonin production. Teenagers aren't staying up late to be difficult—their circadian rhythms naturally delay by 2-3 hours (Carskadon & Acebo, 2002). This biological shift, combined with early school start times, creates chronic sleep deprivation that further narrows the window of tolerance.

Girls typically experience these changes 1-2 years earlier than boys, but both sexes show increased emotional intensity and decreased stress tolerance during pubertal transitions. Understanding this helps parents respond with compassion rather than frustration when their previously easy-going child suddenly seems to overreact to everything.

Identity Development and Emotional Intensity

Adolescence is the time when "Who am I?" becomes the central question of existence. This identity exploration is crucial for healthy development, but it's also emotionally exhausting. Your teenager is essentially trying on different personas to see what fits, and this process naturally creates internal tension and external conflicts.

Erik Erikson identified this stage as "identity versus role confusion" (Erikson, 1968). Teenagers who successfully navigate this stage develop a strong sense of self, while those who struggle may experience prolonged confusion about their identity and role in the world.

The intensity of teenage emotions isn't just about hormones—it's about the monumental task of figuring out who they are and where they belong. Every social interaction, every academic challenge, every family conflict becomes a data point in their identity formation process.

Social media amplifies this natural intensity exponentially. Teenagers are now developing their identities not just within their immediate communities but against the backdrop of global social comparison. The adolescent brain, already hypersensitive to social feedback, gets constant input about how they measure up to idealized versions of their peers.

Dr. Sonia Livingstone's research on digital media and adolescent development shows that social media use can both support and complicate identity formation (Livingstone, 2008). Positive online connections can expand teenagers' sense of possibility, while negative interactions or constant comparison can narrow their window of tolerance and increase anxiety.

The Paradox of Connection and Separation

Teenagers face a fundamental paradox: they need connection more than ever while simultaneously needing to establish independence from their primary attachment figures (their parents). This creates what might seem like contradictory behaviors—seeking comfort from you one moment and pushing you away the next.

Peer relationships become primary co-regulators during adolescence. This shift is developmentally appropriate and necessary.

Your teenager isn't rejecting you personally; they're following a biological imperative to expand their social connections and prepare for adult independence.

However, peer co-regulation comes with risks. Unlike parents who (hopefully) have developed nervous systems and regulation skills, teenage peers are all working with under-construction brains. They can amplify each other's dysregulation rather than providing stabilizing co-regulation.

This is why maintaining connection with your teenager is so crucial, even when they seem to want nothing to do with you. You remain their most important secure base, even if they don't act like it. Your regulated presence provides an anchor point they can return to when peer relationships become overwhelming.

Risk-Taking and Nervous System Seeking

Not all teenage risk-taking is problematic—some of it is necessary for healthy development. The adolescent brain is wired to seek novelty and intensity, which serves important evolutionary purposes. Risk-taking helps teenagers develop independence, learn their limits, and prepare for adult responsibilities.

The key distinction is between **healthy risk-taking** and **harmful risk-taking**. Healthy risks might include trying out for the school play, asking someone to prom, or advocating for a cause they believe in. Harmful risks typically involve immediate physical danger or long-term consequences that teenagers can't fully comprehend due to their still-developing prefrontal cortex.

Dr. Laurence Steinberg's research shows that teenagers take more risks when they're in groups, when they're emotionally aroused, and when they're stressed (Steinberg, 2013). Understanding these triggers helps parents create environments that support healthy risk-taking while minimizing harmful choices.

The teenage nervous system craves intensity and stimulation. This isn't defiance—it's biology. The adolescent brain produces less

114

dopamine at baseline but has an exaggerated response to rewarding stimuli. This creates a neurochemical drive to seek out intense experiences.

When teenagers don't have access to healthy sources of intensity (sports, creative pursuits, meaningful challenges), they may seek stimulation through less healthy means. This is why providing appropriate challenges and adventures is so important during the teenage years.

Understanding Sensation-Seeking

Dr. Marvin Zuckerman's research on sensation-seeking shows that this trait peaks during adolescence and gradually decreases throughout adulthood (Zuckerman, 1994). High sensation-seekers need more intense stimulation to feel satisfied, while low sensation-seekers prefer calmer, more predictable experiences.

Understanding your teenager's sensation-seeking level helps you provide appropriate outlets. High sensation-seekers might thrive with rock climbing, competitive debates, or challenging volunteer work. Lower sensation-seekers might prefer quieter creative pursuits or intimate friendship groups.

The goal isn't to eliminate risk-taking but to channel it constructively. Teenagers who are completely prohibited from taking any risks often engage in more dangerous behaviors when they get the opportunity. Those who have access to appropriate challenges and adventures are more likely to make better choices when faced with potentially harmful situations.

Building Autonomy While Maintaining Connection

The central challenge of parenting teenagers is supporting their growing independence while maintaining enough connection to provide guidance and support. This requires a fundamental shift from external control to collaborative partnership.

Authoritative parenting—high warmth combined with appropriate boundaries—remains the most effective approach during adolescence (Baumrind, 1991). However, what this looks like changes dramatically from the elementary years. The boundaries become more collaborative, and the warmth needs to be expressed in ways that respect your teenager's growing autonomy.

Traditional punishment-based discipline often backfires with teenagers because it threatens their developing sense of autonomy. Instead of compliance, you're more likely to get rebellion. Window of tolerance parenting offers a different approach—one that honors your teenager's developmental needs while still providing the structure and support they need.

Collaborative Problem-Solving

Teenagers need to practice making decisions while still having access to adult wisdom and support. Collaborative problem-solving allows them to develop these skills while knowing they have a safety net.

The process looks different than it did when they were younger. Instead of you identifying problems and solutions, you invite your teenager to notice issues and brainstorm approaches. You provide information and perspective, but they take the lead in developing solutions.

For example, if your teenager is struggling with time management, instead of creating a schedule for them, you might say: "I've noticed you seem stressed about getting everything done. What do you think would help?" Then you work together to identify strategies, with you offering suggestions and resources while they make the final decisions.

This approach accomplishes several important goals simultaneously:

- It respects their growing autonomy
- It builds their problem-solving skills

116

- It maintains your connection and influence

- It allows for natural consequences while providing support

- It reduces power struggles that can damage your relationship

Dialectical Behavior Therapy Skills for Teenagers

DBT (Dialectical Behavior Therapy) skills are particularly valuable for teenagers because they address the core challenges of adolescence: intense emotions, interpersonal conflicts, and the need to balance seemingly contradictory needs.

The four core DBT skill modules translate beautifully to adolescent development:

Distress Tolerance helps teenagers cope with intense emotions without making the situation worse. Skills like the TIPP technique (Temperature, Intense exercise, Paced breathing, Progressive muscle relaxation) provide concrete tools for managing overwhelming feelings.

Emotion Regulation teaches teenagers how to identify, understand, and influence their emotional experiences. This is particularly valuable during adolescence when emotions feel unpredictable and overwhelming.

Interpersonal Effectiveness provides frameworks for maintaining relationships while advocating for their needs. The DEAR MAN technique (Describe, Express, Assert, Reinforce, stay Mindful, Appear confident, Negotiate) gives teenagers concrete tools for difficult conversations.

Mindfulness helps teenagers stay present rather than getting caught up in anxious future thoughts or regretful past experiences. For the adolescent brain, which tends toward emotional extremes, mindfulness provides a crucial anchor point.

Dr. Marsha Linehan's research shows that DBT skills can be effectively adapted for adolescents and significantly improve emotional regulation and interpersonal relationships (Linehan, 2014). Many families find that learning these skills together strengthens their relationships while giving everyone better tools for managing stress.

Technology, Sleep, and Nervous System Health

The adolescent nervous system is particularly vulnerable to the effects of technology and sleep disruption. The same neuroplasticity that makes the teenage brain so adaptable also makes it more susceptible to the negative effects of excessive screen time and poor sleep hygiene.

Research shows that blue light exposure, particularly in the evening, disrupts melatonin production and delays sleep onset (Chang, Aeschbach, Duffy, & Czeisler, 2015). For teenagers, whose circadian rhythms are already naturally delayed, evening screen time can push bedtimes even later and create chronic sleep deprivation.

Sleep deprivation significantly narrows the window of tolerance. When teenagers don't get adequate sleep (9-9.5 hours for most adolescents), they become more emotionally reactive, less able to concentrate, and more likely to engage in risky behaviors (Hirshkowitz et al., 2015).

The relationship between technology use and mental health in adolescents is complex. Moderate use can support social connection and learning, while excessive use, particularly passive consumption of social media, correlates with increased rates of anxiety and depression (Twenge & Campbell, 2018).

Digital Wellness Planning

Rather than blanket technology restrictions, which often create more conflict than compliance, **digital wellness planning involves collaborating with your teenager to create sustainable technology habits that support their nervous system health.**

This process starts with education. Help your teenager understand how their developing brain responds to different types of screen time.

Discuss the difference between active and passive technology use, and how different apps and platforms affect their mood and sleep.

Work together to identify their values and priorities. If they value sleep, academic performance, and face-to-face relationships, help them see how their technology choices either support or undermine these values.

Create agreements rather than rules. Instead of "No phones after 9 PM," you might agree together that phones charge outside bedrooms to support better sleep. Instead of "Only one hour of social media per day," you might agree to check in weekly about how social media use is affecting their mood and adjust as needed.

The goal is to help your teenager develop their own internal awareness and regulation around technology use. This serves them much better in the long run than external controls they'll eventually abandon.

Supporting Academic and Social Challenges

The window of tolerance framework provides valuable perspective on common teenage academic and social struggles. Rather than seeing poor grades or friendship drama as character flaws or defiance, we can recognize them as signs that your teenager's nervous system needs support.

Academic stress can quickly push teenagers outside their window of tolerance. The combination of increased academic demands, social pressures, and biological changes creates a perfect storm for academic struggles. Traditional responses like removing privileges or increasing pressure often make the situation worse by further dysregulating their nervous system.

A window-aware approach to academic challenges involves:

- First addressing nervous system regulation before tackling academic issues

- Creating optimal learning environments that support focused attention

- Building in adequate recovery time between challenging tasks

- Recognizing when to back off versus when to provide gentle encouragement

- Collaborating on strategies rather than imposing solutions

Social Navigation and Peer Relationships

Peer relationships during adolescence carry enormous weight because they serve multiple crucial functions: identity formation, emotional support, social learning, and preparation for adult relationships. This is why friendship drama can feel so devastating to teenagers—these relationships truly matter more than they will at any other life stage.

Social media amplifies both the benefits and risks of peer relationships. Positive online connections can provide support and community, particularly for teenagers who feel different or isolated in their immediate environment. However, cyberbullying, social comparison, and the pressure to maintain an online persona can create chronic stress and narrow the window of tolerance.

Supporting your teenager's social development involves:

- Validating the importance of peer relationships rather than minimizing them

- Teaching skills for healthy relationship boundaries

- Providing guidance without trying to control their friendships

- Creating opportunities for positive social connections

- Helping them recognize and respond to toxic relationship dynamics

Crisis Planning and Professional Support

Every family with a teenager should have a crisis plan. This isn't because you expect a crisis, but because having a plan reduces anxiety for everyone and ensures you're prepared if intense situations arise.

Crisis planning involves identifying:

- Warning signs that your teenager is moving outside their window of tolerance
- Strategies that help them return to regulation
- When to seek immediate professional support
- Emergency contacts and resources
- Your own support system as parents

Professional support isn't just for "serious problems." Many families benefit from working with therapists who specialize in adolescent development, even when there isn't a diagnosed mental health condition. Therapy can provide teenagers with additional tools for emotional regulation and give families neutral space to work through conflicts.

Warning signs that professional support might be helpful include:

- Persistent sleep disruption or dramatic changes in sleep patterns
- Significant changes in appetite or eating behaviors
- Social isolation or withdrawal from previously enjoyed activities
- Academic performance that drops dramatically and doesn't improve with support
- Expressions of hopelessness or thoughts of self-harm
- Substance use or other concerning risk-taking behaviors

- Family conflicts that escalate repeatedly despite your best efforts

Finding the Right Professional Support

Not all therapists are trained in adolescent development or understand the window of tolerance framework. When seeking professional support, look for providers who:

- Have specific training and experience with teenagers
- Use evidence-based approaches like DBT, CBT, or family therapy
- Understand the neuroscience of adolescent development
- Include families in the treatment process when appropriate
- Respect teenagers' growing autonomy while providing necessary structure

Many teenagers are initially resistant to therapy, which is normal and expected. Frame therapy as building life skills rather than "fixing problems." Emphasize that therapy is for people who want to get better at handling life's challenges, not just for people with serious problems.

College Preparation Through a Regulation Lens

The college preparation process can be incredibly stressful for both teenagers and families. The traditional approach of focusing solely on academic achievements and test scores often ignores the emotional and psychological preparation that's equally important for success.

A regulation-focused approach to college preparation includes:

- Building self-awareness about individual learning styles and needs

- Developing independence gradually rather than expecting sudden autonomy

- Teaching self-advocacy skills for academic and social situations

- Creating realistic expectations about the college transition

- Building resilience and stress management skills

- Maintaining family connection while supporting increasing independence

Many students who excel academically in high school struggle in college not because they lack intelligence, but because they lack self-regulation skills. College requires managing time, prioritizing tasks, seeking help when needed, and maintaining social relationships—all while being away from familiar support systems.

Parents can support college readiness by gradually transferring responsibility for academic and life management tasks during the junior and senior years of high school. This might include having your teenager manage their own schedule, handle communication with teachers, and take increasing responsibility for their health and self-care.

Making Decisions About College

The college decision process provides an excellent opportunity to practice collaborative decision-making. Rather than parents making decisions for their teenager or leaving them to figure it out entirely on their own, families can work together to identify values, explore options, and make informed choices.

This process involves helping your teenager:

- Identify their values and priorities for their college experience

- Research schools that align with these values

- Understand the financial implications of different choices

- Visit campuses and ask meaningful questions

- Make the final decision with support but not pressure from family

- Prepare emotionally and practically for the transition

Remember that there's no perfect college choice, and students can succeed in many different environments. The goal is helping your teenager make a thoughtful decision that feels right for them, not finding the "best" school according to external rankings.

Long-Term Perspective: Raising Future Adults

The ultimate goal of parenting teenagers isn't to control their behavior—it's to prepare them for successful independent adulthood. This requires a fundamental shift in perspective from managing their daily choices to building their capacity for self-management.

The window of tolerance framework provides an excellent foundation for this transition. When teenagers understand their own nervous system patterns, they can make better choices about:

- Which environments and activities support their well-being

- How to recognize and respond to their own stress signals

- When to seek support and what kinds of support are most helpful

- How to maintain important relationships while pursuing their goals

- How to recover from setbacks and learn from mistakes

The regulation skills your teenager learns now will serve them throughout their adult life. Every challenge they navigate with your support builds their confidence and competence for handling future difficulties independently.

Trusting the Process

Parenting teenagers requires enormous faith in the long-term process of development. The daily reality of living with a teenager can feel chaotic, unpredictable, and emotionally exhausting. It's easy to lose sight of the bigger picture when you're dealing with daily conflicts about curfews, grades, and responsibilities.

Most teenagers who struggle during adolescence become successful, well-adjusted adults. The intensity of the teenage years doesn't predict adult outcomes. In fact, some research suggests that teenagers who push boundaries and challenge authority may develop stronger leadership skills and more innovative thinking as adults (Dishion, Nelson, & Bullock, 2004).

This doesn't mean accepting disrespectful behavior or dangerous choices. It means understanding that some conflict and struggle during adolescence is normal and healthy. Your job isn't to eliminate all problems but to provide support, guidance, and unconditional love while your teenager figures out who they're becoming.

Real-World Application: The Martinez Family

Let me share how the Martinez family applied these principles when their 15-year-old daughter Sofia began struggling with social anxiety and academic pressure.

Sofia had always been a high achiever and people-pleaser. During her sophomore year, the combination of advanced classes, social media pressure, and friend group changes began pushing her outside her window of tolerance regularly. She became increasingly anxious, started having panic attacks, and began avoiding social situations.

Initially, Sofia's parents responded with traditional approaches: encouraging her to "push through" her anxiety, suggesting she needed to try harder socially, and increasing academic pressure to maintain her grades. These approaches backfired, and Sofia became more withdrawn and anxious.

When they learned about the window of tolerance framework, everything changed. They recognized that Sofia's nervous system was overwhelmed and needed support, not pressure. They worked together to identify her triggers, create calming strategies, and build her distress tolerance skills.

The family implemented several key changes:

They established a "regulation check-in" routine where Sofia rated her stress level each morning and evening. This helped everyone recognize patterns and intervene before she became completely overwhelmed.

They created a "comfort menu" of activities that helped Sofia return to her window of tolerance: taking baths, listening to specific playlists, doing gentle yoga, or having quiet conversations with her mom.

They collaborated with Sofia's school counselor to adjust her course load temporarily while she built better coping skills. Rather than seeing this as failure, they framed it as strategic support for her long-term success.

They worked with a therapist who taught Sofia DBT skills for managing intense emotions and social anxiety. The whole family learned these skills so they could support each other.

Most importantly, they shifted their focus from fixing Sofia's anxiety to supporting her overall nervous system health. They prioritized sleep, nutrition, exercise, and meaningful social connections over academic achievement.

The results weren't immediate, but they were significant. Within six months, Sofia was managing her anxiety more effectively, had rebuilt some important friendships, and was performing well academically without the intense pressure she'd felt before.

More importantly, Sofia developed self-awareness and skills that served her throughout the rest of high school and into college. She learned to recognize her own patterns, advocate for her needs, and seek support when necessary—skills that proved invaluable as she navigated other challenges.

The Martinez family's experience illustrates several key principles:

- **Crisis often signals the need for a different approach, not more of the same**

- **Supporting nervous system health creates the foundation for addressing specific problems**

- **Collaboration and respect for the teenager's autonomy leads to better outcomes than control-based approaches**

- **Professional support can be invaluable during difficult transitions**

- **The skills learned during challenging periods become lifelong assets**

Moving Forward: Your Teen's Regulation Journey

Understanding your teenager's nervous system provides a roadmap for navigating these complex years with more confidence and less conflict. Every teenager's journey is unique, but the principles remain consistent: **regulation first, connection always, and collaboration whenever possible.**

Your teenager needs you now more than ever, even when they act like they don't. Your regulated presence, unconditional love, and faith in their eventual success provide the secure base from which they can explore, make mistakes, and grow into the adults they're meant to become.

The adolescent years are intense for everyone involved, but they're also filled with incredible growth, discovery, and possibility. When you approach these years with nervous system awareness, you're not just helping your teenager survive adolescence—you're helping them develop the emotional intelligence and resilience that will serve them throughout their adult lives.

Remember: you're not trying to eliminate all struggle from your teenager's life. You're providing support and guidance while they learn to navigate challenge and complexity themselves. The window of tolerance framework gives you both a common language and practical tools for this important work.

Trust the process, trust your teenager's innate drive toward health and growth, and trust your own ability to provide the support they need during this remarkable phase of development.

Essential Points for Parents of Teens

The teenage years challenge everything you thought you knew about your child, but understanding the adolescent nervous system provides clarity and hope during these intense years.

Your teenager's brain is literally under construction. The behaviors that frustrate you most—impulsivity, emotional intensity, poor decision-making—reflect biological realities, not character flaws. This knowledge transforms how you respond to daily challenges.

Connection remains your most powerful tool. Even when your teenager seems to want nothing to do with you, your regulated presence provides an essential anchor point. They need to push against something stable and secure as they develop their own identity.

Collaborative approaches work better than control-based discipline. Teenagers have a developmental drive toward autonomy that makes traditional punishment strategies backfire. Working together to solve problems builds their skills while maintaining your relationship.

Professional support is often valuable during adolescence. Therapy, coaching, or family counseling can provide additional tools and neutral space for working through conflicts. Seeking support is a sign of wisdom, not weakness.

The regulation skills your teenager learns now become lifelong assets. Every challenge they navigate with your support builds their capacity for independent adulthood. Your investment in their emotional development pays dividends for decades to come.

Trust the process. Most teenagers who struggle during these years become successful, well-adjusted adults. Your job isn't to eliminate all problems but to provide love, support, and guidance while they figure out who they're becoming.

Chapter 8: When Anxiety Narrows the Window

Supporting Your Worried Child

Eight-year-old Emma had been a confident kindergartener who loved school, friends, and trying new things. But by second grade, something had shifted. Monday mornings became battlegrounds, with Emma clinging to her mother's leg, sobbing that her stomach hurt too much for school. The school nurse found nothing wrong. Her teacher reported that Emma seemed fine once she arrived, though quieter than before.

Emma's parents, David and Maria, tried everything they could think of. They reasoned with her about the importance of education. They offered rewards for good school days. They even tried tough love, dropping her off despite the tears. Nothing worked, and Emma's distress seemed to grow stronger each week.

The breaking point came on a Tuesday morning when Emma locked herself in the bathroom, hyperventilating and saying she felt like she was going to die. That's when David and Maria realized they weren't dealing with defiance or manipulation—they were facing something much more complex and frightening.

Emma's story illustrates how anxiety can completely hijack a child's nervous system, making behaviors that look willful or attention-seeking actually driven by intense fear and physiological distress. For anxious children, what appears to be a simple request—like going to school—can trigger the same fight-flight-freeze response that our ancestors experienced when facing life-threatening dangers.

Understanding anxiety through the window of tolerance framework changes everything about how we respond to worried children. Instead of seeing anxious behaviors as problems to eliminate, we can recognize them as signals that a child's nervous system needs support returning to a regulated state.

Anxiety doesn't just make children feel bad—it literally shrinks their window of tolerance, making them more reactive to all stressors and less able to access their natural problem-solving abilities. This creates a vicious cycle where anxiety leads to avoidance, which reinforces the anxiety, which further narrows the window, leading to more avoidance.

But here's the hopeful truth: **anxiety is highly treatable, especially in children.** When we approach childhood anxiety with nervous system awareness and evidence-based strategies, we can help children expand their windows of tolerance and reclaim their natural confidence and curiosity.

How Anxiety Hijacks the Nervous System

Anxiety is fundamentally a nervous system response, not a character flaw or choice. When children experience anxiety, their brain's alarm system (the amygdala) detects threat—real or perceived—and triggers a cascade of physiological changes designed to help them survive danger.

The anxious child's nervous system interprets neutral or mildly challenging situations as emergencies. A math test becomes a life-or-death situation. A social interaction feels like entering a lion's den. A new experience triggers the same response as encountering a predator.

Dr. Daniel Siegel explains that when the amygdala is activated, it essentially "hijacks" the prefrontal cortex, making rational thought and emotional regulation much more difficult (Siegel, 2012). This is why logical arguments rarely work with anxious children in the moment—their thinking brain is literally offline.

The physical symptoms of anxiety in children are very real and can include rapid heartbeat, sweating, nausea, dizziness, muscle tension, and difficulty breathing. Children often describe these sensations in concrete terms: "My heart is beating out of my chest," "My stomach has butterflies," or "I feel like I can't breathe."

Research shows that children's developing nervous systems are particularly susceptible to anxiety because their prefrontal cortex—the brain region responsible for rational thinking and emotional regulation—won't fully mature until their mid-twenties (Casey, Jones, & Hare, 2008). This means children have fewer internal resources for managing intense emotions and need more external support to return to regulation.

The Biology of Childhood Anxiety

When anxiety activates, several biological systems spring into action simultaneously. The sympathetic nervous system releases stress hormones like cortisol and adrenaline, preparing the body for action. Heart rate increases, breathing becomes shallow, muscles tense, and digestion slows down.

These changes happen automatically and are not under conscious control. Children cannot simply "calm down" on command any more than they can control their heart rate through willpower alone. Understanding this helps parents respond with compassion rather than frustration when children struggle to regulate their anxiety.

Chronic anxiety can lead to persistent activation of these stress systems, which affects sleep, appetite, concentration, and overall health. Children with untreated anxiety often show physical symptoms like frequent stomachaches, headaches, fatigue, and increased susceptibility to illness.

Dr. Bessel van der Kolk's research demonstrates that trauma and chronic stress literally change brain structure and function, particularly in areas responsible for emotional regulation and threat detection (van der Kolk, 2014). While not all childhood anxiety stems from trauma, the same principles apply—persistent anxiety can alter how a child's nervous system functions.

Distinguishing Anxiety from Other Regulation Challenges

Not all emotional distress in children is anxiety, and accurately identifying anxiety is crucial for providing appropriate support. Anxiety has specific characteristics that distinguish it from other regulation challenges like anger, frustration, or sadness.

Core features of childhood anxiety include:

- **Excessive worry** about future events that may never happen

- **Physical symptoms** like stomachaches, headaches, or difficulty breathing

- **Avoidance behaviors** that interfere with daily activities or development

- **Reassurance seeking** that provides only temporary relief

- **Sleep disturbances** including difficulty falling asleep or frequent nightmares

- **Perfectionism** and fear of making mistakes

- **Social withdrawal** from previously enjoyed activities

Anxiety differs from typical childhood fears in several important ways. Normal developmental fears are usually age-appropriate (fear of the dark in preschoolers, fear of performance in school-age children), temporary, and don't significantly interfere with functioning. Anxiety, on the other hand, tends to be persistent, excessive for the situation, and limiting.

Anxiety also differs from attention difficulties, though the two often co-occur. Anxious children may appear inattentive or hyperactive, but their restlessness stems from internal worry rather than difficulty with focus or impulse control. They might check and recheck their work, ask repeated questions for reassurance, or seem

133

unable to concentrate because their minds are occupied with anxious thoughts.

Common Anxiety Presentations by Age

Preschoolers (ages 3-5) typically show anxiety through:

- Separation anxiety that interferes with normal activities
- Extreme clinginess to parents or caregivers
- Regression to earlier behaviors like bedwetting or baby talk
- Repetitive questions seeking reassurance
- Physical complaints without medical cause
- Sleep difficulties including nightmares or resistance to bedtime

School-age children (ages 6-11) often present with:

- School refusal or extreme distress about school attendance
- Perfectionism and fear of making mistakes
- Excessive worry about performance, appearance, or social acceptance
- Physical symptoms that peak during school days
- Difficulty with transitions or changes in routine
- Social withdrawal from peers or activities

Adolescents (ages 12-18) may show:

- Social anxiety that interferes with peer relationships
- Performance anxiety related to academics, sports, or social situations
- Panic attacks or intense physical symptoms of anxiety
- Perfectionism that leads to procrastination or avoidance

- Body image concerns or eating-related anxiety

- Technology-related anxiety including social media pressure

The Anxiety-Avoidance Cycle and Window Shrinking

The relationship between anxiety and avoidance creates a self-perpetuating cycle that progressively narrows a child's window of tolerance. When children avoid situations that trigger their anxiety, they experience immediate relief, which reinforces the avoidance behavior. However, this short-term relief comes at a significant long-term cost.

Each time a child avoids an anxiety-provoking situation, their nervous system learns that the situation is indeed dangerous and should be avoided in the future. This process, called *negative reinforcement*, actually strengthens the anxiety response rather than reducing it.

The cycle typically looks like this:

1. Child encounters or anticipates anxiety-provoking situation

2. Anxiety symptoms activate (physical, emotional, cognitive)

3. Child avoids or escapes the situation

4. Immediate relief reinforces avoidance behavior

5. Anxiety about the situation increases for next time

6. Window of tolerance narrows further

7. More situations become anxiety-provoking

Dr. David Barlow's research on anxiety disorders shows that avoidance is one of the strongest predictors of persistent anxiety (Barlow, 2002). Children who consistently avoid anxiety-provoking situations often see their fears spread to related situations, a process called *generalization*.

For Emma, what started as mild nervousness about a particular teacher generalized to worry about school in general, then to any separation from her parents, and eventually to any unfamiliar situation. Her window of tolerance became so narrow that even minor changes in routine could trigger intense anxiety.

How Avoidance Shrinks the Window

Each avoidance experience sends a message to the nervous system that confirms the perceived danger. The amygdala essentially says, "See? We were right to be afraid. That situation was dangerous, and we barely escaped." This strengthens neural pathways associated with threat detection and weakens pathways associated with safety and coping.

Over time, children may begin avoiding not just the original trigger but anything that reminds them of it. A child who had a panic attack during a math test might start avoiding math class, then school in general, then any situation where they might be evaluated or judged.

The window of tolerance shrinks in multiple dimensions:

- **Sensory tolerance** decreases (normal sounds seem loud, light seems bright)

- **Social tolerance** reduces (familiar people feel overwhelming)

- **Cognitive tolerance** narrows (simple decisions feel impossible)

- **Physical tolerance** diminishes (minor discomfort feels unbearable)

- **Emotional tolerance** contracts (small disappointments feel catastrophic)

This shrinking creates what clinicians call *anxiety sensitivity*—fear of the physical sensations of anxiety itself. Children become afraid not just of the original trigger but of feeling anxious, creating a secondary layer of fear that further complicates treatment.

Building Brave Behaviors Gradually

The antidote to the anxiety-avoidance cycle is gradual, supported exposure to feared situations within the child's expanding window of tolerance. This doesn't mean throwing children into the deep end of their fears—that approach often backfires and can traumatize already vulnerable nervous systems.

Instead, effective anxiety treatment involves carefully titrated experiences that stretch the window of tolerance gradually while maintaining enough safety and support that the child doesn't become overwhelmed. This process is sometimes called *graded exposure* or *systematic desensitization.*

The key principles of building brave behaviors include:

- **Start where the child is,** not where you think they should be

- **Make changes small enough** that success is highly likely

- **Provide abundant support and scaffolding** during challenging moments

- **Celebrate all attempts,** not just successes

- **Move at the child's pace,** not an arbitrary timeline

- **Build on strengths** and previous successes

- **Address the whole nervous system,** not just the specific fear

For Emma, building brave behaviors started not with going to school but with very small steps toward independence. First, she practiced being in a different room from her parents for short periods. Then she spent time at her grandmother's house, which felt safer than school. Gradually, she visited her classroom after school when it was empty, then attended school for just an hour, slowly building up to full days.

The Exposure Hierarchy Within the Window

Effective exposure work requires careful attention to the child's window of tolerance at each step. Exposures that push children too far outside their window can actually increase anxiety and strengthen avoidance patterns. The goal is to find the *sweet spot* where challenge meets support.

Creating an exposure hierarchy involves:

1. **Identifying specific triggers** rather than vague fears

2. **Ranking situations from least to most anxiety-provoking**

3. **Starting with situations that create mild anxiety** (2-3 on a 10-point scale)

4. **Building success experiences** before moving to more challenging situations

5. **Providing coping tools and support** at each level

6. **Celebrating progress** and learning from setbacks

The hierarchy isn't linear—children might need to move back and forth between levels based on their daily regulation, life stressors, and individual progress. Flexibility and responsiveness matter more than rigid adherence to a predetermined plan.

Timing exposures within the window is crucial. When children are already dysregulated from other stressors (poor sleep, family conflict, academic pressure), they have less capacity for managing anxiety-provoking situations. Conversely, when they're well-rested, well-supported, and feeling confident, they can handle bigger challenges.

Cognitive Strategies That Actually Work for Kids

Traditional cognitive-behavioral techniques need significant adaptation to work effectively with children, whose thinking is more concrete and whose emotional regulation abilities are still developing. Abstract concepts like "challenging negative thoughts" often don't resonate with younger children who think in black-and-white terms.

Effective cognitive strategies for anxious children include:

Externalizing the anxiety by giving it a name or character. Many children benefit from personifying their anxiety as "the worry monster," "anxiety brain," or "the what-if bug." This helps them see anxious thoughts as something happening to them rather than an accurate reflection of reality.

Probability estimation using concrete, child-friendly language. Instead of asking children to evaluate the likelihood of their feared outcomes, we might ask, "Has this worry ever actually happened?" or "How many times has going to school been actually dangerous?"

Coping statements that are developmentally appropriate and personally meaningful. Generic phrases like "I can handle this" may not resonate, but personalized statements like "I've done hard things before" or "My family believes in me" can be more powerful.

Problem-solving skills that break overwhelming situations into manageable steps. Anxious children often feel paralyzed by the enormity of their fears, but they can usually identify small, concrete actions they can take.

Worry Time and Worry Postponement

Teaching children to contain their worry to specific times and places can significantly reduce anxiety's interference with daily life. The concept of "worry time" involves scheduling 10-15 minutes daily for focused worrying, while postponing anxious thoughts that arise at other times.

This technique works because it:

- Validates that worry is normal and sometimes useful

- Gives children a sense of control over their anxious thoughts

- Reduces the power of worry by containing it

- Teaches that they don't have to respond to every anxious thought immediately

- Provides structure around an otherwise chaotic experience

Children can keep a "worry box" or "worry journal" where they deposit anxious thoughts throughout the day, knowing they'll address them during worry time. Many find that by the time worry time arrives, their concerns seem less urgent or have resolved themselves.

The key is making worry time structured and time-limited. Children set a timer, focus exclusively on their worries during that period, and then engage in a pleasant, grounding activity afterward. This prevents worry time from becoming another source of anxiety.

Body-Based Anxiety Interventions

Anxiety is fundamentally a physical experience, and body-based interventions often provide faster relief than cognitive strategies alone. Teaching children to work directly with their nervous system through breathing, movement, and sensory techniques can be powerfully effective.

Progressive muscle relaxation adapted for children involves tensing and releasing different muscle groups while using child-friendly imagery. Children might "squeeze like a lemon" and then "melt like ice cream" or "be stiff like a robot" and then "loose like spaghetti."

Breathing techniques must be taught when children are calm, not during anxiety episodes. Simple techniques include:

- **Belly breathing** with one hand on chest, one on belly
- **4-4-4 breathing** (breathe in for 4, hold for 4, out for 4)
- **Birthday candle breathing** (deep breath in, slow breath out like blowing out candles)
- **Flower breathing** (smell the flower slowly, blow the petals gently)

Movement-based interventions can be particularly effective for children who struggle with sitting still during anxiety:

- **Heavy work activities** like pushing against a wall or carrying something heavy

- **Bilateral movements** like cross-lateral marching or dancing

- **Yoga poses** designed for children, particularly grounding poses

- **Sensory activities** like squeezing stress balls or manipulating play dough

Creating Safety Anchors

Safety anchors are specific sensory experiences that help children's nervous systems remember safety and return to regulation. These might include special objects, scents, sounds, or physical sensations that the child associates with calm, safe experiences.

Effective safety anchors are:

- **Portable** so children can access them anywhere

- **Discrete** so they can use them without drawing unwanted attention

- **Personally meaningful** rather than generic

- **Practiced regularly** when calm, not just during crises

- **Sensory-based** to bypass cognitive processing

Examples might include a small smooth stone from a favorite beach, a bracelet that belonged to a beloved grandparent, a particular essential oil scent, or a special song that makes them feel safe and loved.

The power of safety anchors lies in their ability to activate the parasympathetic nervous system (the "rest and digest" response) even in challenging situations. When children practice using these anchors repeatedly during calm moments, they build neural pathways that can be accessed during stress.

When Professional Support Becomes Necessary

Recognizing when childhood anxiety requires professional intervention can be challenging because anxiety exists on a continuum from normal developmental fears to clinical disorders that significantly impair functioning. Several factors can help parents determine when to seek additional support.

Consider professional help when:

- **Daily functioning is significantly impaired** for more than several weeks

- **School attendance becomes consistently problematic** despite supportive interventions

- **Social relationships suffer** due to anxiety-related avoidance

- **Physical symptoms are frequent and interfering** with normal activities

- **Sleep is regularly disrupted** by anxiety or worry

- **Family life is significantly affected** by accommodating the child's anxiety

- **The child expresses hopelessness** or thoughts of self-harm

- **Previous coping strategies stop working** or anxiety seems to be worsening

Dr. Philip Kendall's research on childhood anxiety treatment shows that early intervention leads to better outcomes and can prevent anxiety from becoming more entrenched (Kendall, 2012). Waiting to see if children "grow out of" anxiety often allows patterns to become more established and harder to change.

Different types of professional support may be appropriate depending on the situation:

Child psychologists or therapists trained in evidence-based anxiety treatments can provide individual therapy, family therapy, or group interventions. Look for providers experienced with children and trained in approaches like Cognitive Behavioral Therapy (CBT), exposure therapy, or play therapy.

School counselors or social workers can provide support within the educational setting and coordinate with families and teachers to create appropriate accommodations and interventions.

Pediatricians or child psychiatrists can evaluate whether medication might be helpful as part of a comprehensive treatment plan and can rule out medical causes for physical symptoms.

Finding the Right Professional Match

Not all therapists are equally effective with anxious children, and finding the right match may take some effort. Research shows that the therapeutic relationship is one of the strongest predictors of treatment success, particularly with children who may already be wary of new situations and people.

Look for professionals who:

- Have specific training and experience with childhood anxiety
- Use evidence-based treatments with demonstrated effectiveness
- Involve parents/families in the treatment process appropriately
- Explain their approach in understandable terms
- Seem to genuinely connect with your child
- Respect your family's values and cultural background

- Communicate clearly about treatment goals and progress

Many children benefit from a combination of individual therapy, family sessions, and coordination with school personnel. The most effective treatments address anxiety from multiple angles rather than focusing solely on one approach.

Medication Considerations and Window Expansion

Medication can be a valuable tool for treating childhood anxiety, particularly when symptoms are severe or haven't responded adequately to psychological interventions alone. However, medication decisions require careful consideration of benefits, risks, and individual circumstances.

Research shows that **combining medication with therapy is often more effective than either treatment alone** for moderate to severe childhood anxiety (Walkup et al., 2008). Medication can help expand the window of tolerance enough for children to engage effectively in therapy and practice new coping skills.

Commonly prescribed medications for childhood anxiety include:

Selective Serotonin Reuptake Inhibitors (SSRIs) like sertraline (Zoloft), fluoxetine (Prozac), and fluvoxamine (Luvox) are typically first-line medications for childhood anxiety. These medications are generally well-tolerated and have substantial research support for their effectiveness and safety in children.

Serotonin-Norepinephrine Reuptake Inhibitors (SNRIs) like venlafaxine (Effexor) may be considered when SSRIs aren't effective or well-tolerated.

Short-term anti-anxiety medications like lorazepam (Ativan) are rarely appropriate for children except in very specific circumstances due to risks of dependence and limited long-term effectiveness.

Making Informed Medication Decisions

The decision to use medication should always involve careful consideration of multiple factors including severity of symptoms, impact on functioning, response to non-medication interventions, family history, and individual child factors.

Important considerations include:

- **Severity and impairment:** How significantly is anxiety affecting the child's daily life, relationships, and development?

- **Response to other treatments:** Has therapy been tried and proven insufficient on its own?

- **Family history:** Are there family members who have responded well or poorly to certain medications?

- **Child's age and development:** Younger children may need different considerations than adolescents

- **Side effect profile:** What are the potential risks and benefits for this specific child?

- **Long-term goals:** How does medication fit into the overall treatment plan?

Medication should never be the only intervention for childhood anxiety. Even when medication is helpful, children still need to learn coping skills, practice facing their fears, and address environmental factors that may contribute to their anxiety.

Regular monitoring is essential when children take anxiety medications. This includes tracking both effectiveness (reduction in symptoms, improved functioning) and potential side effects (changes in appetite, sleep, mood, or behavior). Most children who benefit from medication do so within 6-8 weeks of reaching an adequate dose.

School Collaboration for Anxious Children

Schools play a crucial role in supporting anxious children because many childhood fears center around academic and social situations that occur in educational settings. Effective collaboration between families and schools can significantly improve outcomes for anxious children.

School-based support might include:

Environmental accommodations like allowing children to sit near the teacher, use a quiet space when overwhelmed, or have access to a trusted adult during difficult moments.

Academic accommodations such as extended time for tests, alternate testing locations, or modified assignment requirements that reduce anxiety without lowering expectations inappropriately.

Social support including structured lunch activities, peer buddy systems, or small group opportunities that feel safer than large social settings.

Communication systems that allow children to signal when they need support without having to verbalize their distress in front of peers.

Gradual re-entry plans for children returning to school after periods of absence due to anxiety.

Creating Anxiety-Informed Educational Plans

Many anxious children benefit from formal educational plans that document their needs and ensure consistent support across all school personnel. This might include a 504 plan under Section 504 of the Rehabilitation Act or an Individualized Education Program (IEP) if the child qualifies for special education services.

Effective educational plans for anxious children typically include:

- Clear descriptions of how anxiety affects the child's educational experience
- Specific accommodations and modifications that reduce barriers to learning

- Crisis intervention procedures for when anxiety becomes overwhelming

- Communication plans between school and family

- Goals for building independence and coping skills over time

- Regular review and adjustment of the plan based on progress

The most successful school interventions recognize that anxiety is not a choice and that traditional disciplinary approaches are often counterproductive. Instead, they focus on teaching skills, providing support, and gradually building the child's confidence and competence.

Emma's Recovery Journey

Let me return to Emma's story to illustrate how these principles work together in real-world application. After that terrifying Tuesday morning in the bathroom, Emma's parents knew they needed a different approach.

They started by seeking professional support from a child psychologist who specialized in anxiety disorders. The therapist helped them understand that Emma's school refusal wasn't defiance but a genuine nervous system response to perceived threat.

The treatment plan addressed multiple areas simultaneously:

Individual therapy helped Emma learn to identify anxiety in her body, practice coping skills, and gradually face her fears through carefully planned exposure exercises.

Family therapy taught David and Maria how to support Emma without inadvertently reinforcing her avoidance behaviors. They learned to validate her feelings while still maintaining expectations for brave behavior.

School collaboration resulted in accommodations that allowed Emma to start with shortened days, have access to the school counselor when needed, and use a "cue card" system to signal when she needed support.

Nervous system support included improving Emma's sleep hygiene, adding regular physical activity, and teaching the whole family breathing and relaxation techniques.

The progress wasn't linear. There were setbacks, particularly during stressful family periods or when Emma faced new challenges. But gradually, her window of tolerance expanded. She could handle smaller stressors without becoming completely overwhelmed, and she began to trust her own ability to cope with difficult situations.

Within six months, Emma was attending school regularly and had rejoined her soccer team. More importantly, she had developed a toolkit of strategies for managing anxiety and a deeper understanding of her own nervous system patterns.

The key factors in Emma's success included:

- **Understanding anxiety as a nervous system response** rather than a behavioral problem

- **Addressing the whole child** rather than just the specific symptoms

- **Building skills gradually** while providing abundant support

- **Involving all important adults** in her life in the treatment process

- **Maintaining hope and patience** during the challenging periods

- **Celebrating all progress,** not just major milestones

Two years later, Emma still experiences anxiety occasionally, but she has the tools and confidence to manage it effectively. Her parents have also learned to recognize early warning signs and provide appropriate support before anxiety escalates to crisis levels.

Practical Tools for Anxious Families

Families dealing with childhood anxiety benefit from having concrete tools and strategies readily available. Here are some practical resources that many families find helpful:

The Anxiety Tracking Sheet

Helping children notice patterns in their anxiety can reduce its power and help families identify triggers and effective coping strategies. A simple tracking sheet might include:

- Date and time

- Situation or trigger

- Anxiety level (1-10 scale)

- Physical sensations noticed

- Thoughts that came up

- What helped (or didn't help)

- How long the anxiety lasted

This information helps families and professionals identify patterns and adjust support strategies accordingly.

The Worry Box Technique

Many children benefit from having a concrete place to "put" their worries so they don't have to carry them constantly. A worry box can be:

- A decorated shoebox where children write worries on paper and "deposit" them

- A special journal used only for worry thoughts

- A digital app designed for this purpose

- A designated time and place for sharing worries with parents

The key is giving children permission to acknowledge their worries without being consumed by them.

Coping Cards for Different Situations

Portable reminders of coping strategies can be helpful when children are away from home and facing anxiety-provoking situations. Coping cards might include:

- Breathing techniques with simple instructions

- Positive self-talk statements that resonate with the individual child

- Reminder of past successes and brave behaviors

- Contact information for trusted adults

- Sensory grounding techniques they can do anywhere

These cards work best when children help create them during calm moments and practice using them regularly.

Supporting Your Child's Anxious Journey

Parenting an anxious child requires enormous patience, creativity, and faith in your child's capacity for growth and healing. It's easy to become discouraged during difficult periods or to worry that you're not doing enough to help.

The most important things to understand:

Your child's anxiety is not your fault, and recovery is not entirely in your control. Anxiety has multiple contributing factors including genetics, temperament, life experiences, and environmental stressors. While your support is crucial, you cannot single-handedly cure your child's anxiety.

Progress is rarely linear. Children often take two steps forward and one step back, particularly during stressful periods or developmental transitions. Setbacks don't mean the strategies aren't working—they're a normal part of the recovery process.

Small improvements matter. Celebrate when your child tries something new, uses a coping skill, or bounces back more quickly from a difficult moment. These seemingly minor victories build the foundation for larger changes.

Your own regulation is crucial. Children pick up on their parents' anxiety and stress, which can amplify their own nervous system activation. Taking care of your own emotional needs isn't selfish—it's an essential part of supporting your child.

Professional support is a sign of strength, not failure. Many families benefit from working with therapists, counselors, or other professionals who specialize in childhood anxiety. Seeking help shows your commitment to your child's wellbeing.

The goal isn't to eliminate all anxiety but to help your child develop the skills and confidence to manage anxiety when it arises. Some anxiety is normal and even helpful—it keeps us safe and motivates us to prepare for challenges.

With patience, appropriate support, and evidence-based strategies, most anxious children can learn to manage their symptoms effectively and go on to lead full, successful lives. The window of tolerance that seems so narrow today can expand dramatically with time, support, and practice.

Your anxious child has many strengths—sensitivity, empathy, attention to detail, conscientiousness—that will serve them well throughout life. The same nervous system that creates vulnerability to anxiety also contributes to many positive qualities. With your support and the right tools, your child can learn to harness their sensitivity as a strength while managing its challenges effectively.

Supporting Your Anxious Child Through Understanding

Childhood anxiety can feel overwhelming for both children and families, but understanding anxiety as a nervous system response rather than a character flaw changes everything about how we provide support.

Anxiety literally narrows your child's window of tolerance, making them more reactive to all stressors and less able to access their natural coping abilities. The anxiety-avoidance cycle reinforces itself, but it can be interrupted with the right understanding and strategies.

Building brave behaviors happens gradually, within your child's expanding window of tolerance. Pushing too hard too fast often backfires, while gentle, supported challenges help build confidence and competence over time.

Body-based interventions often provide faster relief than cognitive strategies alone, particularly for younger children. Teaching breathing techniques, movement activities, and sensory tools gives children concrete ways to influence their nervous system state.

Professional support can be invaluable for moderate to severe anxiety, and seeking help early often leads to better outcomes. The right therapist can provide both individual skill-building and family support.

School collaboration is often essential since many childhood fears center around academic and social situations. Working with teachers and counselors creates consistency across your child's environments.

Your own regulation matters enormously. Children's nervous systems are constantly influenced by the adults around them. Taking care of your own emotional needs helps you provide the calm, stable presence your anxious child needs.

Most importantly, anxiety is highly treatable, especially in children. With patience, appropriate support, and evidence-based strategies, your child can develop the skills and confidence to manage anxiety effectively and reclaim their natural curiosity and courage.

Chapter 9: ADHD, Autism, and Sensory Differences

Neurodivergent Windows

Ten-year-old Leo was having the worst day of his life, and it wasn't even 10 AM yet. The morning had started with his usual routine disrupted—his favorite breakfast cereal was gone, his regular clothes were in the wash, and the construction noise from next door felt like jackhammers inside his skull. By the time he arrived at school, his nervous system was already running on empty.

The final straw came during math class when the fluorescent light above his desk started flickering. For most kids, this would be a minor annoyance. For Leo, whose autism made him hypersensitive to visual stimuli, it was torture. The irregular flashing triggered what looked like a complete behavioral meltdown—he threw his pencil across the room, knocked over his chair, and began crying inconsolably.

His teacher, Ms. Rodriguez, had two choices. She could see this as defiant behavior requiring discipline, or she could recognize it as a nervous system overwhelmed beyond its capacity to cope. Fortunately, Ms. Rodriguez understood something crucial: **Leo's brain worked differently, and so did his window of tolerance.**

Instead of sending Leo to the principal's office, she dimmed the classroom lights, offered him noise-canceling headphones, and gave him space to regulate in the quiet corner they'd set up together. Within ten minutes, Leo was calm enough to communicate that the flickering light had made him feel "like his brain was breaking." They moved his desk, and he finished his math worksheet successfully.

This scenario illustrates something essential about neurodivergent children: **their windows of tolerance operate differently than**

neurotypical children's, requiring adapted strategies and deeper understanding of their unique nervous system needs.

Leo's story could have ended with punishment, shame, and further dysregulation. Instead, it became a learning opportunity that strengthened his relationship with his teacher and built his confidence in his ability to recover from overwhelming moments. The difference lay in understanding neurodivergence through the lens of nervous system awareness rather than behavioral compliance.

Understanding Neurodivergent Nervous Systems

Neurodivergence isn't a deficit—it's a different way of processing the world that comes with both unique challenges and remarkable strengths. The term *neurodivergent*, coined by sociologist Judy Singer, encompasses conditions like ADHD, autism, dyslexia, and other neurological differences that affect how the brain processes information (Singer, 1999).

For neurodivergent children, the window of tolerance often has different dimensions and requires different types of support to maintain optimal functioning. Understanding these differences is crucial for parents, teachers, and others who want to support neurodivergent children effectively.

ADHD brains are wired for novelty-seeking and struggle with sustained attention to non-preferred activities. Dr. Russell Barkley's research shows that ADHD is fundamentally a disorder of executive function—the brain's management system responsible for planning, organizing, and regulating behavior (Barkley, 2015). Children with ADHD often have windows of tolerance that fluctuate dramatically based on interest level, time of day, and environmental factors.

Autistic nervous systems process sensory information differently, often with heightened sensitivity or reduced sensitivity in various domains. Dr. Temple Grandin's work has helped us understand that autistic individuals may experience the world with sensory intensity that neurotypical people can't imagine—sounds seem louder, lights appear brighter, and textures feel more intense (Grandin, 2006).

Both ADHD and autism frequently involve sensory processing differences that significantly impact the window of tolerance. A child might be hypersensitive to certain stimuli (sounds, textures, lights) while being hyposensitive to others (proprioceptive input, vestibular stimulation). This creates a complex sensory profile that affects how they experience and interact with their environment.

The Neurodivergent Window of Tolerance

Traditional approaches to behavior management often fail with neurodivergent children because they don't account for the different ways these nervous systems operate. What looks like defiance or lack of motivation may actually be a nervous system operating outside its optimal zone.

For ADHD children, the window of tolerance is often narrower in several key areas:

- Sustained attention to non-preferred tasks
- Tolerance for boring or repetitive activities
- Ability to transition between activities smoothly
- Capacity for sitting still during passive learning
- Emotional regulation when frustrated or overwhelmed

For autistic children, the window of tolerance may be particularly narrow around:

- Sensory experiences that feel overwhelming or unpredictable
- Social interactions that require complex communication
- Changes in routine or unexpected transitions
- Environments with multiple competing stimuli

- Situations requiring flexible thinking or problem-solving

However, it's crucial to understand that **these same children often have remarkably wide windows of tolerance for their areas of interest and strength.** An ADHD child who can't sit still during a history lesson might focus intensely on building with Legos for hours. An autistic child who struggles with casual conversation might demonstrate exceptional knowledge and sustained attention when discussing their special interests.

Sensory Processing and Window Tolerance

Sensory processing differences are central to understanding most neurodivergent children's windows of tolerance. Dr. A. Jean Ayres pioneered our understanding of sensory processing disorder, showing how children who can't effectively process sensory information struggle with regulation, learning, and behavior (Ayres, 2005).

The eight sensory systems (not just the traditional five) each play a role in nervous system regulation:

1. **Visual** - processing what we see

2. **Auditory** - processing sounds and noise

3. **Tactile** - processing touch and texture

4. **Gustatory** - processing taste

5. **Olfactory** - processing smell

6. **Vestibular** - processing movement and balance

7. **Proprioceptive** - processing body position and spatial awareness

8. **Interoceptive** - processing internal body signals like hunger, thirst, and need for the bathroom

Neurodivergent children often have mixed sensory profiles, being hypersensitive (over-responsive) in some areas while being hyposensitive (under-responsive) in others. This creates unique challenges for maintaining regulation throughout the day.

Hypersensitivity and Window Narrowing

When children are hypersensitive to certain sensory inputs, those inputs can quickly push them outside their window of tolerance. Common hypersensitivities include:

- **Auditory sensitivity** to background noise, sudden sounds, or specific frequencies

- **Tactile sensitivity** to clothing textures, food textures, or unexpected touch

- **Visual sensitivity** to bright lights, flickering lights, or busy visual environments

- **Olfactory sensitivity** to perfumes, cleaning products, or food smells

- **Movement sensitivity** that makes car rides or playground activities overwhelming

These sensitivities aren't preferences or pickiness—they're neurological differences that create genuine distress. A child who covers their ears and melts down in a noisy restaurant isn't being dramatic; their nervous system is genuinely overwhelmed by auditory input that others find tolerable.

Hyposensitivity and Regulation Needs

Children who are hyposensitive to certain inputs often seek more intense stimulation to help their nervous systems reach optimal functioning. This might look like:

- **Proprioceptive seeking** through rough play, heavy lifting, or crashing into furniture

- **Vestibular seeking** through spinning, swinging, or other movement activities

- **Tactile seeking** through touching everything or preferring tight hugs and heavy blankets

- **Auditory seeking** through making loud noises or needing music to concentrate

Rather than viewing these behaviors as disruptive, we can understand them as the child's attempt to regulate their nervous system and reach their optimal window of tolerance.

Executive Function Challenges and Regulation

Executive function skills—planning, organizing, working memory, and emotional regulation—are often affected in neurodivergent children. Dr. Thomas Brown's model of executive function describes six key clusters that impact daily functioning: activation, focus, effort, emotion, memory, and action (Brown, 2013).

For many neurodivergent children, executive function challenges directly impact their ability to maintain regulation. They might:

- Struggle to initiate tasks even when they want to complete them

- Have difficulty estimating how long activities will take

- Forget important steps in multi-step processes

- Become overwhelmed when trying to organize their thoughts or materials

- Have intense emotional reactions to minor frustrations

- Struggle to shift attention from preferred to non-preferred activities

These challenges aren't about intelligence or motivation—they're about brain differences that affect the neural networks responsible for managing complex tasks and emotional regulation.

Working Memory and Overwhelm

Working memory—the ability to hold and manipulate information mentally—is often affected in neurodivergent children. This creates particular challenges in academic and social situations where children need to process multiple pieces of information simultaneously.

A child might understand each individual direction but become overwhelmed when given multi-step instructions. They might know the math concept but struggle to complete problems that require holding several steps in mind at once. These working memory challenges can quickly push children outside their window of tolerance, particularly in demanding academic environments.

Supporting working memory reduces cognitive load and helps children stay within their optimal functioning zone. This might include:

- Breaking complex tasks into smaller, sequential steps
- Providing visual supports and checklists
- Reducing background distractions that compete for attention
- Teaching children to externalize information through writing or drawing
- Building in processing time between instructions

The Critical Importance of Predictability and Routine

For many neurodivergent children, predictability and routine aren't just preferences—they're essential for nervous system regulation. When the world feels unpredictable or chaotic, these children use enormous amounts of mental energy just trying to anticipate what might happen next.

Routine provides several regulatory benefits:

- Reduces anxiety by making the day more predictable
- Conserves mental energy for learning and social interaction

- Creates a sense of safety and control

- Helps children develop independence through practiced patterns

- Provides structure that supports executive function challenges

Dr. Barry Prizant's research on autism emphasizes that what might look like "rigidity" is often a child's adaptive strategy for managing a world that feels overwhelming and unpredictable (Prizant, 2015). The child who insists on taking the same route to school isn't being stubborn—they're reducing cognitive load so they can focus their energy on learning.

Transitions as Regulation Challenges

Transitions between activities are particularly challenging for many neurodivergent children because they require multiple executive function skills simultaneously: stopping one activity, shifting attention, predicting what comes next, and starting something new.

Effective transition support includes:

- **Advance warning** with specific time markers ("In five minutes, we'll clean up")

- **Visual schedules** that show what's happening throughout the day

- **Transition objects or rituals** that provide comfort during changes

- **Processing time** to mentally prepare for the switch

- **Consistent routines** that make transitions more predictable

Many families find that investing time in creating smooth transition routines dramatically reduces daily stress and conflict for everyone.

Advocating for Accommodations

Neurodivergent children often need environmental modifications and support strategies to access their education and participate fully in family and community life. These accommodations aren't "special treatment"—they're necessary supports that level the playing field.

Common accommodations for ADHD children might include:

- **Movement breaks** or fidget tools to support attention

- **Preferential seating** away from distractions

- **Modified assignments** that maintain academic standards while reducing overwhelming elements

- **Extra time** for processing and completing tasks

- **Organizational supports** like visual schedules and checklists

- **Clear expectations** and consistent routines

Accommodations for autistic children often focus on:

- **Sensory modifications** like alternative lighting or noise reduction

- **Communication supports** including visual aids and processing time

- **Social supports** such as structured interaction opportunities

- **Predictability** through schedules and advance notice of changes

- **Sensory breaks** when overstimulation occurs

The Difference Between Accommodations and Modifications

Understanding the distinction between accommodations and modifications helps families advocate effectively. *Accommodations* change how a child accesses learning without changing what they're expected to learn. *Modifications* change what the child is expected to learn or demonstrate.

Most neurodivergent children benefit primarily from accommodations that support their learning style and nervous system needs rather than modifications that lower academic expectations. The goal is helping them show what they know and can do, not reducing standards.

Celebrating Neurodivergent Strengths

The same brain differences that create challenges also contribute to remarkable strengths. Neurodivergent individuals often demonstrate exceptional abilities in pattern recognition, creative problem-solving, attention to detail, innovative thinking, and passionate expertise in their interest areas.

Common ADHD strengths include:

- **Creativity and innovative thinking** that generates novel solutions

- **Hyperfocus abilities** when engaged with interesting material

- **High energy and enthusiasm** that can be contagious

- **Risk-taking and entrepreneurial thinking** that leads to breakthroughs

- **Empathy and emotional sensitivity** that supports deep relationships

- **Resilience and adaptability** developed through overcoming challenges

Autistic strengths often include:

- **Attention to detail** that catches things others miss

- **Systematic thinking** that excels at analyzing patterns

- **Honesty and authenticity** that builds trust

- **Deep expertise** in areas of special interest

- **Logical thinking** that isn't swayed by social pressures

- **Reliability and consistency** when systems are in place

Focusing on strengths isn't about ignoring challenges—it's about building a complete picture of the child that includes both their support needs and their remarkable abilities. Children who understand their strengths alongside their challenges develop healthier self-concepts and greater resilience.

Interest-Based Learning and Regulation

Many neurodivergent children's areas of intense interest can become powerful tools for regulation and learning. Rather than viewing special interests as distractions from "real" learning, we can harness them as bridges to skill development and nervous system regulation.

A child fascinated with trains might learn math through calculating train schedules, develop writing skills by creating train stories, and practice social skills by sharing their expertise with others. These interests often represent areas where the child's window of tolerance is naturally wide, making them ideal starting points for building confidence and skills.

Sensory Diet Planning

A sensory diet is a personalized plan of sensory activities designed to help a child maintain optimal arousal and regulation throughout the day. Just as we plan meals to meet nutritional needs, we can plan sensory experiences to meet nervous system needs.

Effective sensory diets are:

- **Individualized** based on the child's specific sensory profile

- **Proactive** rather than just reactive to problems

- **Integrated** into daily routines rather than separate activities

- **Flexible** and adjusted based on daily needs and responses

164

- **Collaborative** involving input from the child, family, and professionals

A typical sensory diet might include:

Morning activities to help the nervous system wake up and organize:

- Heavy work like carrying a backpack or doing wall push-ups
- Proprioceptive input through jumping or stretching
- Organizing activities that provide calming deep pressure

Midday regulation during transitions or challenging periods:

- Movement breaks between sedentary activities
- Calming sensory input like deep breathing or soft music
- Alerting input like crunchy snacks or cool water

Evening wind-down to prepare for sleep:

- Calming activities like warm baths or gentle massage
- Reduced sensory stimulation in the environment
- Predictable routines that signal bedtime

Creating Sensory Tools and Spaces

Having access to appropriate sensory tools helps children regulate independently and builds their confidence in managing their own needs. These tools should be:

- **Portable** so they can be used in different settings
- **Socially acceptable** for the child's age and environment
- **Easy to use** independently
- **Effective** for the individual child's needs
- **Available** when needed without lengthy explanations

Examples of effective sensory tools:

- Fidget items that provide proprioceptive or tactile input

- Noise-canceling headphones for auditory sensitivity

- Weighted lap pads for calming deep pressure

- Chewelry for children who seek oral input

- Essential oil rollers for calming scents

- Compression clothing for proprioceptive support

Sensory spaces at home and school provide children with designated areas for regulation. These might include quiet corners with soft lighting, movement areas with therapy balls or swings, or organized spaces with clearly defined boundaries and purposes.

Visual Supports for Regulation

Many neurodivergent children are visual learners who benefit from seeing information rather than just hearing it. Visual supports can reduce anxiety, support memory and organization, and help children understand expectations and routines.

Effective visual supports include:

Daily schedules that show the sequence of activities with pictures or words, helping children anticipate what's coming and feel more in control of their day.

Task analyses that break complex activities into simple, visual steps, supporting executive function challenges and building independence.

Emotion regulation charts that help children identify their feelings and select appropriate coping strategies.

Social stories that explain social situations, expectations, and appropriate responses in concrete, visual terms.

Choice boards that provide options for activities, snacks, or coping strategies, supporting autonomy while maintaining structure.

Making Visual Supports Effective

Visual supports work best when they're:

- **Meaningful** to the individual child
- **Current** and updated regularly
- **Accessible** when and where they're needed
- **Age-appropriate** in design and content
- **Functional** rather than just decorative

Many children benefit from participating in creating their own visual supports, which increases buy-in and ensures the supports match their individual needs and preferences.

Movement as Medicine

For many neurodivergent children, movement isn't just enjoyable—it's essential for nervous system regulation. Research shows that physical activity directly impacts brain function, improving attention, mood, and executive function (Ratey & Hagerman, 2008).

Movement serves multiple regulatory functions:

- **Alerting** the nervous system when energy is low
- **Calming** an overactive system through rhythmic, predictable activities
- **Organizing** sensory input through proprioceptive and vestibular stimulation
- **Focusing** attention through bilateral coordination activities
- **Releasing** tension and built-up energy

Different types of movement serve different regulatory purposes:

Heavy work activities like carrying, pushing, or pulling provide proprioceptive input that's often calming and organizing. Examples include carrying books, doing wall push-ups, or helping with household chores that involve lifting or moving.

Linear movement like swinging or rocking can be calming for overstimulated nervous systems, while **rotary movement** like spinning is often alerting and energizing.

Bilateral coordination activities that cross the midline of the body support brain integration and can improve focus and learning readiness.

Integrating Movement into Daily Life

Rather than viewing movement as separate from learning or daily activities, we can integrate regulatory movement throughout the day. This might include:

- **Movement breaks** every 20-30 minutes during sedentary activities

- **Active learning** that incorporates movement into academic tasks

- **Transition activities** that use movement to help shift between activities

- **Household responsibilities** that provide proprioceptive input

- **Outdoor time** that offers natural movement opportunities

Many families find that prioritizing daily movement significantly reduces challenging behaviors and improves overall family harmony.

Communication Adaptations

Neurodivergent children often have unique communication needs that extend beyond traditional speech and language considerations.

These might include differences in processing time, social communication challenges, or alternative communication preferences.

Supporting communication includes:

Processing time - Many neurodivergent children need extra time to process language and formulate responses. Allowing wait time after questions or instructions reduces pressure and improves communication success.

Clear, concrete language - Abstract concepts, idioms, and figurative language can be confusing. Direct, specific language is often more effective.

Visual communication supports - Some children communicate better through pictures, writing, or typing than through speech, particularly when stressed or overwhelmed.

Reduced language during stress - When children are dysregulated, their language processing abilities often decrease. Simple, key words are more effective than lengthy explanations.

Alternative communication methods - Some children benefit from augmentative and alternative communication (AAC) devices, sign language, or written communication, either temporarily or permanently.

Supporting Social Communication

Social communication involves more than just speaking—it includes understanding social cues, taking turns in conversation, reading body language, and adjusting communication based on the social context. Many neurodivergent children need explicit instruction and practice in these skills.

Social communication support might include:

- Teaching conversation skills through structured practice
- Explaining social rules that might not be intuitive

- Providing scripts or frameworks for common social situations

- Creating opportunities for positive social interaction

- Teaching self-advocacy skills for communicating their needs

The goal isn't to make neurodivergent children indistinguishable from their neurotypical peers, but to help them communicate effectively and build meaningful relationships in their own authentic way.

Leo's Regulation Journey

Let's return to Leo's story to see how these principles work together in practice. After that difficult morning in math class, Leo's team—including his parents, teacher, and occupational therapist—worked together to develop a comprehensive support plan.

They started by conducting a thorough sensory assessment to understand Leo's specific triggers and needs. They discovered that Leo was particularly sensitive to fluorescent lights and sudden loud noises, while he sought proprioceptive input through movement and deep pressure.

His sensory diet included:

- **Morning activities** like jumping on a trampoline before school to help organize his nervous system

- **Classroom accommodations** including preferential seating away from fluorescent lights and access to a weighted lap pad

- **Movement breaks** every 30 minutes during academic work

- **Quiet space access** when he felt overwhelmed

- **Transition warnings** five minutes before changes in activities

Visual supports helped Leo understand expectations and feel more in control:

- A daily visual schedule showing the sequence of activities

- A "regulation thermometer" to help him identify his energy level

- Choice cards for coping strategies when he felt overwhelmed

- Social stories explaining classroom routines and expectations

Communication adaptations included:

- Extra processing time after instructions

- Written backup for verbal directions

- Permission to request clarification without feeling embarrassed

- A signal system with his teacher for when he needed support

Most importantly, Leo's team focused on building his self-awareness and self-advocacy skills. They taught him to recognize his own sensory needs, communicate them appropriately, and implement coping strategies independently.

Within a few months, Leo's meltdowns became much less frequent. More importantly, he developed confidence in his ability to handle challenging situations and pride in his unique strengths, including his exceptional attention to detail and creative problem-solving abilities.

The key elements of Leo's success included:

- Understanding his behavior as communication about his nervous system needs

- Providing proactive support rather than just reacting to problems

- Building on his strengths while addressing his challenges

- Teaching him to understand and advocate for himself

- Creating collaborative partnerships between home and school

- Maintaining high expectations while providing necessary supports

Technology Tools for Neurodivergent Regulation

Technology can provide valuable support for neurodivergent children's regulation and learning when used thoughtfully and strategically. The key is finding tools that support the child's individual needs rather than adding more complexity to their lives.

Helpful regulation apps might include:

- **Timer apps** that provide visual countdowns for transitions and activities

- **Mood tracking apps** that help children identify patterns in their regulation

- **Breathing apps** that guide calming exercises with visual and auditory cues

- **Organization apps** that support executive function challenges

- **Communication apps** for children who benefit from AAC support

Educational technology can also support regulation by:

- Allowing children to work at their own pace

- Providing multi-sensory input through visual, auditory, and tactile elements

- Offering immediate feedback and reinforcement

- Breaking complex tasks into manageable steps

- Providing choice and control over learning environment

Balancing Technology Use

While technology can be helpful, it's important to balance screen time with other regulatory activities like movement, social interaction, and hands-on learning. Some neurodivergent children may hyperfocus on technology to the exclusion of other important activities, requiring supportive limits and alternative options.

The goal is using technology as one tool in a comprehensive support system, not as a replacement for human connection and real-world experiences.

Building Independence and Self-Advocacy

The ultimate goal of supporting neurodivergent children is helping them understand their own needs and develop skills for self-advocacy and independence. This process starts early with helping children recognize their own patterns and builds toward adult self-determination.

Building self-awareness includes:

- Teaching children about their neurological differences in positive, strengths-based ways

- Helping them identify their own sensory preferences and triggers

- Building emotional vocabulary to describe their internal experiences

- Recognizing the connection between their environment, activities, and regulation

Self-advocacy skills include:

- Communicating their needs clearly and appropriately

- Requesting accommodations or modifications when necessary

- Choosing appropriate coping strategies for different situations

- Understanding their rights and protections under disability law
- Building confidence in their ability to navigate challenges

Independence building involves:

- Gradually transferring responsibility for regulation strategies from adults to the child
- Teaching problem-solving skills for novel situations
- Building resilience and flexibility while maintaining necessary supports
- Preparing for transitions between different life stages and environments

Creating Neurodiversity-Affirming Environments

Truly supportive environments for neurodivergent children go beyond individual accommodations to embrace neurodiversity as a natural and valuable part of human variation. This means creating spaces, systems, and cultures that work for different kinds of brains from the start.

Neurodiversity-affirming practices include:

- **Universal design** that anticipates different needs rather than requiring individual requests
- **Strength-based approaches** that highlight what children do well
- **Flexible expectations** that allow for different ways of demonstrating knowledge and ability
- **Respectful communication** that values neurodivergent perspectives and experiences
- **Inclusive communities** where differences are seen as contributions rather than problems

In families, this might look like:

- Family meetings that include all perspectives and communication styles

- Household routines that accommodate different sensory and organizational needs

- Celebration of each family member's unique strengths and interests

- Problem-solving approaches that consider multiple viewpoints and solutions

In schools, neurodiversity-affirming practices include:

- Classroom design that provides multiple seating and learning options

- Teaching methods that engage different learning styles simultaneously

- Assessment options that allow children to show knowledge in various ways

- Social learning that teaches neurotypical children about neurodiversity

- Discipline approaches that focus on understanding and problem-solving rather than punishment

Looking Toward the Future

Neurodivergent children grow into neurodivergent adults who can make exceptional contributions to their communities and society. Many of our greatest innovations, artistic achievements, and scientific breakthroughs have come from individuals who think differently.

Supporting neurodivergent children effectively involves:

- Understanding their unique nervous system patterns and needs

- Providing appropriate accommodations and modifications

- Building their self-awareness and self-advocacy skills

- Celebrating their strengths alongside addressing their challenges

- Creating environments that embrace neurodiversity

- Preparing them for successful, authentic adult lives

The goal isn't to make neurodivergent children "normal"—it's to help them become confident, capable, and authentic versions of themselves. When we understand and support their unique windows of tolerance, we create opportunities for them to thrive in ways that honor both their challenges and their remarkable strengths.

Leo's story continues as he develops into a confident young person who understands his own needs, advocates for appropriate support, and uses his unique abilities to contribute meaningfully to his community. His early struggles with regulation became the foundation for building resilience, self-awareness, and pride in his neurodivergent identity.

The same can be true for every neurodivergent child when we approach them with understanding, respect, and commitment to supporting their authentic development and success.

Supporting Your Neurodivergent Child's Unique Window

Neurodivergent children's windows of tolerance operate differently than neurotypical children's, requiring adapted strategies that honor their unique nervous system patterns while building on their remarkable strengths.

Understanding neurodivergent nervous systems means recognizing that behaviors that look challenging or defiant often represent attempts to regulate an overwhelmed or under-stimulated system. ADHD and autistic brains process the world differently, creating both vulnerabilities and exceptional abilities.

Sensory processing differences significantly impact most neurodivergent children's windows of tolerance. Mixed sensory profiles—being hypersensitive in some areas while being hyposensitive in others—create complex regulatory needs that require individualized support strategies.

Executive function challenges affect planning, organization, and emotional regulation, directly impacting the ability to maintain optimal functioning. Supporting these skills through external structure and explicit teaching helps expand the window of tolerance.

Predictability and routine aren't rigidity for neurodivergent children—they're essential regulatory supports that conserve mental energy for learning and social interaction. Smooth transitions and clear expectations reduce overwhelm and build confidence.

Accommodations level the playing field by removing barriers that prevent neurodivergent children from accessing their education and demonstrating their abilities. These supports don't lower expectations—they provide alternative ways to meet high standards.

Neurodivergent strengths deserve equal attention to challenges. The same brain differences that create difficulties also contribute to creativity, attention to detail, innovative thinking, and passionate expertise that benefit families, schools, and communities.

Building self-awareness and self-advocacy skills prepares neurodivergent children for successful, authentic adult lives. When they understand their own patterns and needs, they can communicate effectively and make informed choices about their support and environment.

The goal isn't to make neurodivergent children indistinguishable from their peers—it's to help them become confident, capable versions of themselves who can navigate the world successfully while honoring their unique neurology.

Chapter 10: Healing from Trauma

Rebuilding Safety and Expanding Windows

Twelve-year-old Malik had been in foster care for three years, moving through six different placements before arriving at Sarah and James's home. His caseworker warned them about his "behavioral issues"— aggressive outbursts, hoarding food, difficulty sleeping, and what seemed like deliberate defiance of household rules. Previous foster families had labeled him "difficult" and "ungrateful."

Sarah and James had a different lens. They understood trauma.

On Malik's first morning, Sarah found him awake at 5 AM, fully dressed, with his few belongings packed in a garbage bag beside his bed. When she gently asked what was happening, he looked at her with eyes much older than his twelve years and said, "I know I messed up yesterday. You can call my worker now."

What had Malik done to "mess up"? He'd eaten three helpings at dinner—the first consistent meal he'd had in weeks—and asked if he could have seconds on dessert. To him, this felt like taking too much, being greedy, crossing an invisible line that had triggered placement disruptions before.

This moment crystallized something essential about trauma-informed parenting: what looks like misbehavior is often a child's nervous system trying to survive in a world that has taught them that safety is temporary and adults can't be trusted.

Instead of calling the caseworker, Sarah sat on Malik's bed and said quietly, "Malik, you didn't mess up. You're safe here. We're not sending you away because you ate dinner or asked for dessert. That's what growing kids are supposed to do."

It took six months for Malik to stop packing his bag every few days. It took a year for him to believe that having seconds at dinner wouldn't result in punishment or rejection. But gradually, his window of tolerance—which trauma had compressed to nearly nothing—began to expand as he learned that this home operated differently than his previous experiences had taught him to expect.

How Trauma Affects the Developing Nervous System

Trauma fundamentally alters how the nervous system develops and functions, particularly when it occurs during childhood when the brain is most malleable. Dr. Bessel van der Kolk's groundbreaking research shows that trauma literally changes brain architecture, affecting areas responsible for emotional regulation, memory processing, and threat detection (van der Kolk, 2014).

Childhood trauma exists on a spectrum from single-incident events like accidents or natural disasters to complex, ongoing experiences like neglect, abuse, or household dysfunction. The Adverse Childhood Experiences (ACE) study, one of the largest investigations into childhood abuse and neglect ever conducted, found that traumatic experiences are far more common than previously understood and have profound long-term effects on health and behavior (Felitti et al., 1998).

The developing brain prioritizes survival over learning when faced with ongoing threat or unpredictability. This means that children who've experienced trauma often have nervous systems that are hypervigilant to danger, quick to react with fight, flight, or freeze responses, and slow to trust that safety is genuine.

Trauma affects the window of tolerance in several ways:

- **Hyperarousal** becomes the default state, with children existing in chronic fight-or-flight activation

- **Hypoarousal** may alternate with hyperarousal, causing children to shut down emotionally or dissociate

180

- **The optimal zone** becomes extremely narrow, making it difficult to stay regulated in everyday situations

- **Recovery time** from dysregulation extends significantly, with children struggling to return to baseline

The Trauma Response System

The trauma response involves three key brain areas that become dysregulated when children experience ongoing threat or unpredictability:

The brainstem controls basic survival functions like heart rate, breathing, and sleep. Trauma can cause chronic activation of these systems, leading to sleep disturbances, digestive issues, and hypervigilance.

The limbic system processes emotions and memories. In traumatized children, this system often becomes hypersensitive to threat, triggering intense emotional reactions to minor stressors that remind them of past dangers.

The neocortex handles higher-order thinking, language, and executive functions. When the lower brain areas are activated by trauma responses, the thinking brain goes offline, making it difficult for children to access rational thought, language, or problem-solving skills.

Dr. Bruce Perry's research demonstrates that trauma affects children differently depending on when it occurs during development (Perry, 2006). Early trauma affects more primitive brain functions, while later trauma may have more impact on higher-order thinking and emotional regulation.

Understanding this brain science helps us recognize that trauma behaviors aren't choices—they're adaptations. The child who hoards food learned that resources might disappear without warning. The child who flinches at loud noises has a nervous system trained to detect danger. The child who lies about small things learned that truth-telling wasn't always safe.

Safety as the Foundation for Window Expansion

For children who've experienced trauma, felt safety must be established before any other therapeutic work can be effective. This isn't just physical safety—though that's essential—but *felt safety*, the deep internal knowing that they are protected, valued, and secure.

Felt safety develops through consistent, predictable experiences of care, protection, and attunement. It can't be achieved through words alone but requires repeated experiences that contradict the child's trauma-learned expectations about relationships and the world.

The components of felt safety include:

Physical safety - The basic knowledge that their body is protected from harm, they will have adequate food and shelter, and adults will not hurt them.

Emotional safety - The experience of having their feelings validated rather than criticized, with adults remaining calm even when the child is dysregulated.

Relational safety - Learning that relationships can be trustworthy, that adults will keep their promises, and that connection doesn't inevitably lead to abandonment or betrayal.

Psychological safety - The freedom to be authentic, make mistakes, express needs, and exist without constant vigilance or performance demands.

Building Safety Through Consistency

For traumatized children, consistency isn't just helpful—it's therapeutic. Every time a caregiver follows through on a promise, maintains a routine, or responds predictably to the child's needs, they're providing evidence that contradicts the child's trauma-learned beliefs about relationships and safety.

Trauma-informed consistency includes:

- Following through on both promises and reasonable consequences

- Maintaining routines even when the child tests them

- Responding to dysregulation with calm stability rather than escalation

- Showing up emotionally even when the child pushes away

- Providing the same message through multiple modalities (words, actions, presence)

This doesn't mean being rigid or never adjusting approaches. It means being reliably trustworthy and emotionally available, even when the child's trauma symptoms make this challenging.

Understanding Trauma Behaviors vs. Willful Defiance

One of the most important shifts in trauma-informed parenting is understanding the difference between trauma responses and willful defiance. This distinction changes everything about how we respond to challenging behaviors.

Trauma behaviors are driven by nervous system activation and serve protective functions, even when they seem illogical or inappropriate. These behaviors developed to help the child survive in dangerous or unpredictable environments.

Common trauma behaviors include:

Hypervigilance - Constant scanning for danger, difficulty relaxing, startled responses to normal sounds or movements.

Control-seeking - Needing to know what's happening next, resistance to transitions, difficulty with surprises or changes in plans.

Regression - Returning to earlier developmental behaviors when stressed, such as bedwetting, baby talk, or clinging.

Emotional dysregulation - Intense reactions to minor frustrations, difficulty recovering from upset, emotions that seem disproportionate to the situation.

Dissociation - "Checking out" mentally during stress, appearing spaced out or disconnected, not responding to their name.

Somatic complaints - Frequent stomachaches, headaches, or other physical symptoms without clear medical cause.

Sleep disturbances - Difficulty falling asleep, frequent nightmares, or wanting to sleep in unusual places.

Willful Defiance vs. Trauma Response

Willful defiance involves a child who:

- Understands expectations and consequences clearly
- Has the cognitive and emotional capacity to comply
- Chooses not to follow directions as a power struggle
- Can be redirected through consistent limits and natural consequences
- Shows defiance across multiple relationships and settings

Trauma responses involve a child who:

- May understand expectations cognitively but can't access that understanding when triggered
- Has a nervous system that perceives threat even in safe situations
- Reacts from a place of survival rather than conscious choice
- Needs co-regulation and safety-building before behavioral change is possible
- May show different behaviors with different caregivers based on their sense of safety

The key difference is that trauma behaviors serve a protective function and persist because they once helped the child survive. These behaviors won't change through traditional discipline because they aren't under conscious control.

The Power of Repetition and Patience

Healing from trauma requires thousands of small, positive interactions that slowly convince the nervous system that safety is real and lasting. Dr. Perry's research shows that the brain changes through "repetitive, relevant, and rewarding experiences" that create new neural pathways (Perry, 2006).

This means that trauma recovery is measured in:

- Months and years rather than days and weeks

- Small improvements rather than dramatic breakthroughs

- Two steps forward and one step back progress patterns

- Building internal resources rather than eliminating all symptoms

- Developing new responses rather than simply stopping old ones

The repetition required for trauma healing is different from typical learning because it must override deeply ingrained survival patterns. A child might need hundreds of experiences of adults staying calm during their meltdowns before they begin to trust that dysregulation doesn't lead to abandonment.

Understanding Trauma Time

Traumatized children often have a different relationship with time that affects their ability to trust that good things will continue or that bad things won't return. They may:

- Live in "trauma time" where past dangers feel present and immediate

- Have difficulty believing that current safety will continue into the future

- Experience hypervigilance that makes time feel slow and threatening

- Struggle with memory formation that makes positive experiences feel less real than traumatic ones

Healing happens in "safety time," where consistent, positive experiences gradually convince the nervous system that the present is different from the past and that the future can be trusted.

This process can't be rushed, and it often involves what seems like backward progress when children test safety through challenging behaviors. These tests aren't defiance—they're the child's way of asking, "Are you really going to stay calm and caring when I'm at my worst?"

Secondary Trauma and Family Systems

Caring for a traumatized child creates stress for the entire family system and can lead to secondary trauma in caregivers, siblings, and extended family members. Understanding and addressing these impacts is essential for maintaining the stability needed for trauma recovery.

Secondary trauma symptoms in caregivers might include:

- Emotional exhaustion and compassion fatigue

- Hypervigilance about the child's safety and wellbeing

- Difficulty sleeping due to worry or the child's sleep disturbances

- Social isolation as family activities become challenging

- Relationship stress as partners cope differently with trauma behaviors

- Physical symptoms like headaches, digestive issues, or muscle tension

Siblings may experience:

- Confusion about why the traumatized child gets "special treatment"
- Fear or anxiety related to the traumatized child's behaviors
- Guilt about their own easier childhood experiences
- Resentment about changed family dynamics or reduced attention
- Their own trauma symptoms from witnessing family stress

Family Trauma-Informed Approaches

Supporting the whole family system requires:

Education about trauma's effects so all family members understand that challenging behaviors aren't personal attacks or choices.

Individual support for each family member to process their own experiences and develop coping strategies.

Family therapy that addresses the impact of trauma on relationships and teaches healthy communication and conflict resolution skills.

Respite care that gives primary caregivers breaks to recharge and maintain their own regulation.

Community support through trauma-informed support groups, respite providers, and understanding friends and family.

Self-care systems that prioritize caregiver physical and emotional health as essential to the child's recovery.

Creating Felt Safety

Felt safety develops through consistent experiences of attunement, protection, and care that gradually convince the child's nervous system that they are truly secure. This process requires both external safety measures and internal experiences of being seen, understood, and valued.

Practical elements of felt safety include:

Predictable routines that help the child know what to expect and feel in control of their environment.

Consistent caregivers who show up emotionally and remain stable even during the child's dysregulated moments.

Choice and control within safe boundaries, allowing the child to make decisions about their daily experiences whenever possible.

Sensory comfort through weighted blankets, soft textures, calming scents, or other sensory inputs that soothe the nervous system.

Connection rituals like bedtime stories, special breakfast routines, or one-on-one time that builds positive associations with relationships.

Physical safety measures that address the child's specific fears or triggers, such as night lights, locks on doors, or ways to contact caregivers.

Attunement and Co-Regulation

Attunement—the ability to sense and respond to another person's emotional state—is central to building felt safety with traumatized children. Dr. Daniel Siegel describes attunement as "feeling felt" by another person (Siegel, 2012).

Trauma-informed attunement involves:

- Noticing the child's emotional state without judgment
- Reflecting their experience back to them with empathy
- Staying regulated yourself even when the child is dysregulated

- Offering comfort and support without trying to "fix" their feelings

- Being present and available without overwhelming the child with intensity

Co-regulation—helping another person return to a regulated state through your own calm presence—is often more effective than teaching self-regulation skills to children whose nervous systems are still learning that safety is possible.

Predictability as Medicine

For children whose early experiences were chaotic or unpredictable, routine and structure serve a therapeutic function. Predictability allows the nervous system to relax its constant vigilance and begin to trust that needs will be met consistently.

Trauma-informed predictability includes:

Daily routines that remain consistent even when other things change, helping the child feel grounded and secure.

Advance warning about changes or transitions, giving the child time to mentally prepare and maintain their sense of control.

Ritual and tradition that create positive anticipation and belonging, such as special holiday traditions or weekly family activities.

Consistent responses to the child's behaviors, so they can predict how caregivers will react and feel safe to be authentic.

Reliable presence of key caregivers, with clear communication about when separations will occur and when reunions will happen.

Flexibility Within Structure

Trauma-informed structure is firm but not rigid. While consistency is essential, children also need to learn that change can be safe and that they can adapt to new situations without losing their sense of security.

This might involve:

- Maintaining core routines (meals, bedtime, connection time) while allowing flexibility in other areas

- Teaching coping strategies for when plans change unexpectedly

- Gradually introducing positive changes to build confidence in the child's adaptability

- Having backup plans and safety nets when trying new experiences

- Celebrating successful navigation of changes, however small

The goal is helping the child develop internal flexibility while maintaining external predictability.

Regression as Healing

Many traumatized children show regression—returning to earlier developmental behaviors—as part of their healing process. Understanding regression as potentially therapeutic rather than concerning helps caregivers respond supportively.

Regression serves several functions:

- Allows the child to experience the safety and care they missed during earlier developmental stages

- Provides comfort during times of stress or overwhelming growth

- Helps the nervous system reorganize and integrate traumatic experiences

- Creates opportunities for caregivers to meet dependency needs that weren't met previously

- Builds attachment relationships through nurturing experiences

Common regression behaviors include:

- Wanting to be fed, bathed, or dressed despite having independent skills

- Using baby talk or younger vocabulary

- Increased clinginess or separation anxiety

- Bedwetting or other toileting accidents

- Wanting comfort items like stuffed animals or blankets

- Needing more physical comfort and reassurance

Responding to Regression Therapeutically

Trauma-informed responses to regression involve:

Meeting the child where they are rather than pushing them to act their chronological age.

Providing nurturing care without shame or pressure to "grow up."

Recognizing regression as communication about the child's current emotional needs.

Balancing dependency needs with age-appropriate expectations in other areas.

Consulting with trauma-informed professionals when regression interferes significantly with functioning or persists without improvement.

Understanding that healing isn't linear and that regression may come and go as the child processes their experiences.

The key is responding to regression with curiosity and compassion rather than concern or correction.

Building Trust Slowly

Trust develops incrementally for traumatized children, often through a series of small interactions rather than dramatic gestures. Children who've experienced betrayal by caregivers need extensive evidence that relationships can be safe before they risk genuine vulnerability.

Trust-building involves:

Keeping small promises consistently, such as saying you'll be back in ten minutes and returning exactly when promised.

Following through on both positive and negative consequences so the child learns that your words have meaning.

Staying emotionally available even when the child tests the relationship through challenging behaviors.

Respecting the child's boundaries while maintaining necessary safety limits.

Being honest about difficult topics in age-appropriate ways, avoiding false reassurance or promises you can't keep.

Showing up during difficult moments rather than withdrawing when the child is struggling.

The Testing Phase

Most traumatized children will test new relationships to see if caregivers will abandon, punish, or reject them when they show their authentic selves. This testing often looks like:

- Escalating challenging behaviors shortly after placement or during times of increased closeness

- Pushing boundaries to see if consequences are consistent and fair

- Showing their "worst" behavior to caregivers they're beginning to trust

- Verbal rejections like "You're not my real parent" or "I hate you"

- Attempts to control the relationship through manipulation or withdrawal

Understanding testing as communication helps caregivers respond therapeutically:

- "I see you're checking to make sure I'm really going to stay calm when you're upset."

- "It makes sense that you'd want to know if I'm going to keep caring about you even when you make mistakes."

- "You're testing our relationship to see if it's really safe. That's actually pretty smart."

The goal is passing these tests by remaining stable, caring, and consistent even when the child's behavior is challenging.

Therapeutic Parenting Techniques

Therapeutic parenting combines traditional parenting with trauma-informed strategies that address the underlying nervous system dysregulation driving challenging behaviors. These approaches prioritize connection and co-regulation while still maintaining appropriate boundaries and expectations.

Core therapeutic parenting principles include:

Connection before correction - Addressing the child's emotional state and underlying needs before focusing on behavior modification.

Regulation before reasoning - Helping the child return to a calm state before engaging in problem-solving or teaching.

Relationship as the foundation - Using the caregiver-child relationship as the primary tool for healing and growth.

Trauma lens for behaviors - Understanding challenging behaviors as adaptations or communications rather than defiance.

Patience with the process - Accepting that healing takes time and that progress isn't always linear.

Specific Therapeutic Techniques

Time-in instead of time-out - Staying close to provide co-regulation during dysregulated moments rather than isolating the child when they most need connection.

Felt safety check-ins - Regularly asking about the child's internal experience and adjusting support based on their feedback.

Narrative therapy approaches - Helping the child develop a coherent story about their experiences that includes both trauma and resilience.

Body-based interventions - Using movement, breathing, and sensory strategies to help the nervous system return to regulation.

Playful engagement - Using humor, games, and fun interactions to build positive associations with relationships and reduce stress.

Collaborative problem-solving - Including the child in finding solutions to challenges, respecting their expertise about their own experiences.

Malik's Healing Journey

Returning to Malik's story shows how these principles work together over time. His healing journey illustrates both the challenges and possibilities of trauma-informed parenting.

The first six months were the hardest. Malik tested every boundary, hoarded food despite consistent meals, and had explosive reactions to minor changes in routine. Sarah and James focused on:

- Maintaining predictable daily routines

- Staying calm during his emotional storms

- Following through on small promises consistently

- Providing sensory comfort during dysregulated moments

- Seeking support for their own secondary trauma symptoms

Months 6-12 brought gradual improvements. Malik stopped packing his bag nightly but still kept important belongings easily accessible. He began asking for help with homework but would quickly shut down if frustrated. His foster parents:

- Celebrated small victories without overwhelming him with attention

- Continued providing structure while allowing more choices

- Began introducing positive changes gradually

- Started family therapy to address relationship dynamics

- Maintained connections with trauma-informed support networks

Year two showed significant progress. Malik began talking about his past experiences, formed a friendship at school, and started sleeping through the night consistently. He still struggled with transitions and had occasional meltdowns, but he recovered more quickly and began using coping strategies independently.

By year three, Malik had developed secure attachment relationships and was functioning well academically and socially. He still had trauma symptoms during times of stress, but he understood his triggers and had effective strategies for managing them. Most importantly, he had internalized the message that he was worthy of love and care.

The key elements of Malik's success included:

- Caregivers who understood trauma and remained committed through difficult periods

- Professional support that included both individual and family therapy

- A school team that implemented trauma-informed approaches

- Consistent, therapeutic responses to challenging behaviors

- Patience with the long-term nature of trauma recovery

- Celebration of progress while accepting ongoing needs

When to Seek Trauma-Informed Therapy

Professional support is often essential for children healing from trauma and for families navigating the complex dynamics of trauma recovery. Knowing when to seek help and what to look for in trauma-informed services can significantly impact outcomes.

Consider professional support when:

- The child shows persistent trauma symptoms that interfere with daily functioning

- Family relationships are significantly strained by trauma-related behaviors

- Caregivers experience secondary trauma symptoms that affect their ability to provide stable support

- The child engages in self-harm or expresses thoughts of suicide

- Trauma symptoms aren't improving despite consistent trauma-informed approaches

- School or legal systems are involved and need professional guidance

- Multiple placements or relationship disruptions have occurred

Effective trauma-informed therapy typically includes:

- Assessment of trauma history and current symptoms

- Evidence-based treatments like Trauma-Focused Cognitive Behavioral Therapy (TF-CBT) or Eye Movement Desensitization and Reprocessing (EMDR)

- Family therapy that addresses the impact of trauma on relationships

- Caregiver support and education about trauma-informed parenting

- Coordination with schools and other systems involved in the child's life

- Regular evaluation of progress and adjustment of treatment approaches

Finding Trauma-Informed Professionals

Not all therapists are trained in trauma-informed approaches, and finding the right professional match can take time and effort. Look for providers who:

- Have specific training in childhood trauma and attachment

- Use evidence-based trauma treatments

- Understand the impact of trauma on brain development

- Include families in the treatment process

- Coordinate with other systems (schools, medical providers, child welfare)

- Demonstrate cultural competence and sensitivity

- Show understanding of the complex nature of trauma recovery

Many communities have specialized trauma programs or agencies that focus specifically on serving children and families affected by trauma.

Self-Care for Trauma Caregivers

Caring for traumatized children is demanding work that requires extraordinary emotional, physical, and psychological resources. Without adequate self-care, caregivers risk burnout, secondary trauma, and their own dysregulation—which ultimately affects their ability to provide the stable, consistent support traumatized children need.

Essential self-care elements include:

Professional support through therapy, support groups, or coaching that addresses the unique challenges of trauma parenting.

Physical care including regular exercise, adequate sleep, nutritious meals, and medical care for stress-related symptoms.

Emotional support from friends, family, or support groups who understand the realities of trauma parenting.

Respite care that provides regular breaks from caregiving responsibilities to recharge and maintain perspective.

Spiritual or meaning-making practices that provide strength and hope during difficult periods.

Education and training that builds confidence and competence in trauma-informed approaches.

Managing Secondary Trauma

Secondary trauma—the emotional distress that results from caring for someone who has been traumatized—is a common experience for trauma caregivers. Recognizing and addressing secondary trauma is essential for both caregiver wellbeing and the child's recovery.

Signs of secondary trauma include:

- Intrusive thoughts about the child's traumatic experiences

- Hypervigilance about the child's safety

- Difficulty sleeping or concentrating

- Emotional numbing or detachment

- Increased anxiety or depression

- Physical symptoms like headaches or digestive issues

- Relationship problems with partners, friends, or family

Managing secondary trauma involves:

- Recognizing symptoms as normal responses to difficult circumstances

- Seeking professional support when symptoms interfere with functioning

- Building strong support networks with others who understand trauma parenting

- Practicing stress management techniques like meditation, yoga, or deep breathing

- Setting appropriate boundaries to protect emotional energy

- Engaging in activities that bring joy and restoration

Creating Trauma-Informed Family Cultures

Families healing from trauma benefit from intentionally creating cultures that prioritize safety, connection, and growth for all family members. This involves examining family values, communication patterns, and daily practices through a trauma-informed lens.

Trauma-informed family cultures typically include:

Safety as the top priority in all decisions and interactions, with physical and emotional safety taking precedence over convenience or social expectations.

Open communication about feelings, needs, and experiences, with validation and empathy as standard responses.

Flexibility and adaptability that allows for changes in plans or approaches based on family members' regulation and needs.

Celebration of small victories and recognition of progress, effort, and growth in addition to achievements.

Conflict resolution skills that address underlying needs and maintain relationships even during disagreements.

Shared activities that build positive memories and strengthen family bonds without pressure or performance expectations.

Building Resilience Together

Trauma-informed families focus on building collective resilience rather than just managing problems. This involves:

- Identifying and building on family strengths and resources

- Creating meaning and purpose from difficult experiences

- Developing family narratives that include both challenges and growth

- Building connections with supportive community members and organizations

- Teaching all family members skills for managing stress and supporting each other

- Maintaining hope and optimism about the family's future

These approaches benefit all family members and create environments where healing is possible for everyone.

Long-Term Recovery and Growth

Trauma recovery is possible, and children can not only heal but thrive when they receive appropriate support and care. While trauma leaves lasting impacts, it doesn't have to define a child's future or limit their potential for happiness and success.

Successful long-term recovery typically includes:

- Development of secure attachment relationships
- Integration of traumatic experiences into coherent life narratives
- Effective strategies for managing triggers and stress
- Strong social connections and support networks
- Academic, vocational, or creative achievements that build confidence
- Ability to form healthy relationships and trust appropriately
- Resilience and post-traumatic growth

Children who heal from trauma often develop exceptional strengths including empathy, resilience, creativity, and the ability to help others who have faced similar challenges. Many become advocates, helpers, or leaders who use their experiences to benefit their communities.

The journey of trauma recovery continues throughout life, with new challenges and growth opportunities at different developmental stages. The foundation of safety, connection, and trust built during childhood provides the base for ongoing healing and development.

Malik's story continues as he moves through adolescence and young adulthood with secure attachment relationships, effective coping strategies, and a strong sense of his own worth and potential. His early trauma experiences became part of his story but not the defining element of his identity.

The same possibility exists for every child when we understand trauma through the lens of nervous system science and respond with the patience, consistency, and care that healing requires.

Supporting Healing Through Trauma-Informed Care

Trauma fundamentally alters how children's nervous systems develop and function, but recovery is possible when caregivers understand these impacts and respond with trauma-informed approaches that prioritize safety and connection.

Trauma behaviors serve protective functions and aren't willful defiance. Children who hoard food, test boundaries, or have emotional meltdowns are responding to past experiences that taught them the world was dangerous and adults couldn't be trusted.

Felt safety must be established before other healing work can be effective. This requires thousands of small, consistent experiences of care, protection, and attunement that gradually convince the nervous system that security is real and lasting.

Repetition and patience are essential because trauma recovery happens slowly through "repetitive, relevant, and rewarding experiences" that build new neural pathways. Healing is measured in months and years, not days and weeks.

Secondary trauma affects entire family systems, requiring support for all family members to maintain the stability needed for the traumatized child's recovery. Caregiver self-care isn't selfish—it's essential.

Therapeutic parenting combines traditional parenting with trauma-informed strategies that prioritize connection before correction and use relationships as the primary tool for healing.

Professional support is often necessary for both traumatized children and their families. Look for trauma-informed providers who use evidence-based treatments and understand the complex nature of trauma recovery.

Long-term recovery is possible when children receive consistent, trauma-informed care. While trauma leaves lasting impacts, it doesn't have to define children's futures or limit their potential for happiness and success.

The window of tolerance that trauma has compressed can expand through experiences of safety, connection, and care, allowing children not just to survive but to thrive.

Chapter 11: Daily Dysregulation Dilemmas

Practical Solutions for Common Scenarios

Monday morning, 7:15 AM: Five-year-old Anna screams that her socks "feel wrong" while her mom frantically searches for the "right" pair, knowing they'll be late for school again.

Tuesday evening, 8:30 PM: Seven-year-old Marcus throws his math homework across the room, sobbing that he's "stupid" while his dad feels his own frustration rising.

Wednesday afternoon, 3:45 PM: Nine-year-old twins Sophia and Isabella erupt into a physical fight over who gets to use the iPad first, both completely dysregulated from their long school day.

Thursday at the grocery store: Three-year-old Zoe has a complete meltdown in the cereal aisle while other shoppers stare and her embarrassed father wonders if he should just leave his cart and go home.

Friday night, 10 PM: The Chen family is still battling bedtime with six-year-old Lucas, who's had four glasses of water, needed six different stuffed animals, and is now crying about monsters under his bed.

Sound familiar? These scenarios play out in millions of homes every day, leaving parents feeling frustrated, children feeling misunderstood, and families stuck in cycles of stress and conflict.

Here's the thing most parenting advice misses: these aren't discipline problems or character defects. They're nervous system regulation challenges that require completely different responses than traditional behavioral approaches. When we understand daily conflicts through the window of tolerance lens, we can transform these moments from battles into opportunities for connection and skill-building.

This chapter provides specific strategies for the most common dysregulation dilemmas families face. Rather than generic advice that works for some children sometimes, you'll get targeted approaches that address the nervous system patterns underlying each challenge.

Because here's the truth: **when you change how you respond to dysregulation, you change your child's experience of their own emotions and your family's entire dynamic.**

Morning Routine Meltdowns

Morning meltdowns aren't about children being "difficult"— they're about nervous systems that haven't yet organized for the day ahead. Sleep transitions affect regulation, hunger impacts mood, and the pressure to get ready quickly can push children outside their window of tolerance before they've even had breakfast.

The nervous system science behind morning struggles:

After eight to twelve hours of rest, children's nervous systems need time to "come online" and organize for the day. The transition from sleep to wakefulness affects neurotransmitter function, blood sugar levels, and stress hormone production. Rushing this process often backfires, creating dysregulation that affects the entire day.

Research shows that cortisol levels naturally rise in the morning to help us wake up and feel alert (Adam et al., 2006). However, children who are already stressed or who have sensitive nervous systems may experience this cortisol increase as anxiety or irritability rather than alertness.

Creating regulation-friendly mornings involves:

Starting the night before by preparing clothes, backpacks, and breakfast options when everyone is calm and thinking clearly.

Building in extra time so the morning doesn't feel rushed or pressured, allowing children's nervous systems to wake up gradually.

Predictable routines that reduce decision-making demands when cognitive resources are limited.

Sensory supports like soft lighting, calm music, or favorite breakfast foods that help the nervous system organize positively.

Connection before tasks through brief snuggling, reading together, or sharing breakfast before diving into the getting-ready routine.

The CALM Morning Method

C - Connect first: Start with physical affection, eye contact, or shared quiet time before discussing the day's plans.

A - Assess regulation: Notice your child's energy level and adjust expectations accordingly. Some mornings require slower pacing or modified routines.

L - Limit choices: Offer simple options (blue shirt or red shirt) rather than overwhelming decisions (what do you want to wear today).

M - Move mindfully: Build movement into the routine through dancing while getting dressed, animal walks to the bathroom, or stretching together.

For Anna's sock struggles, her mom learned to prepare three acceptable sock options the night before and to validate Anna's sensory experience ("These socks do feel different") while problem-solving together ("Let's find ones that feel good on your feet").

Bedtime Battles and Nervous System Wind-Down

Bedtime resistance often signals a nervous system that hasn't successfully transitioned from the day's activation to the calm state needed for sleep. Traditional approaches that focus on compliance ("Just go to bed!") miss the underlying regulation challenges that make sleep feel impossible or unsafe.

The neuroscience of sleep preparation:

The transition to sleep requires activation of the parasympathetic nervous system—the "rest and digest" response that calms heart rate, relaxes muscles, and slows brain activity. Children who've been overstimulated during the day may struggle to access this calming response.

Melatonin production, which signals sleepiness, can be disrupted by screen time, bright lights, exciting activities, or stress. Dr. Marc Weissbluth's research shows that overtired children often become more alert and hyperactive rather than sleepy, making bedtime even more challenging (Weissbluth, 2005).

Sleep-supportive nervous system practices:

Wind-down routines that begin 1-2 hours before actual bedtime, gradually reducing stimulation and increasing calming activities.

Sensory preparation through dim lighting, soft pajamas, calming scents, or white noise that signals the nervous system to prepare for rest.

Connection rituals like reading together, gentle massage, or quiet talking that provide co-regulation and security.

Addressing specific fears through comfort objects, night lights, or reassurance strategies that help children feel safe in their bedrooms.

Consistent timing that works with children's natural circadian rhythms rather than fighting them.

The Bedtime Regulation Routine

Two hours before bed: Begin reducing stimulation through dimmer lights, calmer activities, and transition away from screens.

One hour before bed: Start physical preparation (bath, teeth, pajamas) combined with calming sensory input.

Thirty minutes before bed: Quiet connection time through reading, gentle conversation, or relaxation activities.

Bedtime: Brief, consistent routine that signals sleep time without extended negotiations or stimulating activities.

For Lucas's bedtime battles, his parents realized he was using delay tactics because he felt anxious about separating at night. They created a "bedtime basket" with water, tissues, and comfort items he might need, eliminating most reasons to get up. They also implemented a brief check-in system where they returned for a quick reassurance after ten minutes, gradually extending the time as Lucas felt more secure.

Sibling Conflicts and Multiple Windows Colliding

Sibling conflicts are often the result of multiple nervous systems operating at different regulation levels, creating perfect storms of dysregulation that escalate quickly. Understanding each child's window of tolerance helps parents intervene effectively rather than just managing the aftermath.

The nervous system dynamics of sibling conflict:

Children's regulation states are contagious—one child's dysregulation can quickly spread to siblings through mirror neuron activation and emotional contagion. Dr. Daniel Siegel's research on family systems shows that family members' nervous systems influence each other constantly (Siegel, 2020).

Age differences create different window sizes and triggers. A toddler's need for immediate gratification conflicts with a school-age child's sense of fairness. A teenager's need for autonomy clashes with a younger sibling's desire for connection.

Competition for caregiver attention can trigger survival-based behaviors, particularly in children who've experienced inconsistent care or attention.

Different temperaments and sensory needs create conflicts when one child's regulation strategy interferes with another's. The child who needs quiet to focus conflicts with the sibling who needs movement and sound to regulate.

Preventing Sibling Dysregulation Spirals

Proactive regulation support often prevents conflicts from escalating into full family chaos:

Individual check-ins that assess each child's regulation level and provide targeted support before problems arise.

Space and time management that ensures each child has access to regulation resources without competing with siblings.

Clear family rules about respecting others' regulation needs, such as quiet time for the sensitive child or movement breaks for the active child.

Problem-solving together during calm moments to address recurring conflicts and develop solutions that work for everyone.

Celebrating cooperation and mutual support when siblings help each other regulate or solve problems together.

For Sophia and Isabella's iPad battles, their parents created a visual timer system where each child got designated time, eliminating arguments about fairness. They also established "transition warnings" five minutes before switches, giving children time to finish their current activity and mentally prepare for the change.

Public Meltdowns and Portable Co-Regulation

Public meltdowns feel especially challenging because they combine child dysregulation with parent embarrassment and social pressure. Understanding that meltdowns signal nervous system overwhelm—not defiance—helps parents respond therapeutically even in public spaces.

Why public spaces trigger meltdowns:

Sensory overload from crowds, noise, bright lights, or unfamiliar smells can quickly push sensitive children outside their window of tolerance.

Overstimulation from new sights, sounds, and experiences accumulates throughout outings, eventually overwhelming the child's capacity to cope.

Reduced predictability in public spaces makes it harder for children to feel in control and safe.

Parent stress about behavior and social judgment can increase family tension and reduce co-regulation capacity.

Fatigue and hunger compound regulation challenges, making children more vulnerable to triggers.

The Portable Regulation Toolkit

Successful public outings require advance planning and portable tools that help children stay within their window of tolerance:

Sensory tools like noise-canceling headphones, sunglasses, fidget items, or chewy jewelry that help children manage overwhelming input.

Comfort objects such as small stuffed animals, family photos, or special items that provide emotional grounding.

Snacks and water to maintain blood sugar and hydration, preventing hunger-related dysregulation.

Exit strategies that allow families to leave situations that become overwhelming without shame or pressure.

Connection activities like hand-holding, quiet singing, or simple games that provide co-regulation during challenging moments.

Scripts and signals that help children communicate their needs without having to verbalize complex emotions in public.

For Zoe's grocery store meltdown, her father learned to recognize early warning signs of overstimulation and began shopping during less busy times, bringing snacks and a small toy, and setting clear expectations about the shopping trip's length and purpose.

Homework Resistance and After-School Regulation

After-school homework battles often stem from children whose nervous systems are depleted from the day's demands and who lack the regulation resources needed for additional cognitive work. Understanding this transforms how families approach homework time.

The after-school regulation challenge:

Children spend 6-8 hours in structured environments that require significant self-regulation resources. By afternoon, many children are running on empty, making additional demands feel overwhelming.

Transition from school to home requires shifting from external structure to family routines, which can be jarring for children who thrive on predictability.

Academic fatigue affects attention, memory, and frustration tolerance, making homework feel much harder than it would with a regulated nervous system.

Social exhaustion from peer interactions can leave children with little capacity for family interactions or academic tasks.

The After-School Regulation Protocol

Step 1: Decompress (15-30 minutes) Allow children to transition from school mode through physical activity, snack time, or quiet sensory input that helps their nervous system settle.

Step 2: Connect (10-15 minutes) Spend focused time together without agenda—listening to their day, offering physical affection, or sharing a snack together.

Step 3: Assess (5 minutes) Check their regulation level and energy capacity before making homework demands.

Step 4: Support (as needed) Provide environmental modifications, break tasks into smaller chunks, or offer co-regulation during challenging work.

Step 5: Celebrate (5 minutes) Acknowledge effort and progress, not just completion, building positive associations with learning.

For Marcus's homework meltdowns, his parents instituted a "homework snack and chat" time where Marcus could decompress and connect before attempting academic work. They also created a calm homework space with fidget tools and background music, and broke assignments into 15-minute chunks with movement breaks between sections.

Screen Time Transitions and Digital Regulation

The transition from screen time to other activities creates regulation challenges because digital media often provides intense sensory input and dopamine stimulation that makes "real world" activities feel boring or understimulating by comparison.

How screens affect the nervous system:

Dr. Anna Lembke's research shows that digital media can create dopamine spikes similar to addictive substances, leading to tolerance and withdrawal-like symptoms when access is removed (Lembke, 2021). This explains why children often become dysregulated when screen time ends, regardless of how much warning they receive.

Blue light exposure affects circadian rhythms and can increase alertness at times when the nervous system should be winding down.

Fast-paced visual input can overstimulate the nervous system, making slower-paced activities feel intolerable.

Social media and gaming often activate stress responses through competition, social comparison, or exciting content that leaves the nervous system in an activated state.

Regulation-Friendly Screen Time Strategies

Before screen time:

- Choose content thoughtfully based on the child's current regulation level

- Set clear time limits using visual timers that children can see

- Plan transition activities that will happen after screen time ends

- Ensure children are fed, hydrated, and reasonably regulated before beginning

During screen time:

- Use co-viewing when possible to maintain connection

- Choose educational or calming content over fast-paced, exciting programs

- Take breaks during longer screen sessions for movement or sensory input

- Monitor children's regulation levels and adjust accordingly

After screen time:

- Provide transition warnings at 10 minutes, 5 minutes, and 1 minute

- Offer alternative activities that provide similar regulation benefits

- Use movement, music, or sensory activities to help the nervous system transition

- Stay nearby to provide co-regulation during the adjustment period

- Avoid scheduling screen time right before activities requiring focus or calm

The key is matching post-screen activities to the child's regulation needs rather than expecting immediate compliance with completely different demands.

Meal Time Struggles and Food Regulation Connections

Food and nervous system regulation are intimately connected through blood sugar stability, sensory experiences, and emotional associations. Many mealtime battles actually reflect regulation challenges rather than pickiness or defiance.

How nutrition affects the window of tolerance:

Blood sugar fluctuations directly impact mood, attention, and emotional regulation. Children who experience blood sugar drops often become irritable, unfocused, or emotionally reactive.

Sensory processing differences affect how children experience food textures, temperatures, smells, and tastes. Children with sensory sensitivities may have genuine difficulty tolerating certain foods.

Stress and appetite are closely linked through the vagus nerve. Stressed or anxious children may lose their appetite or experience digestive issues that affect their relationship with food.

Mealtime environment influences children's ability to focus on eating. Chaotic, rushed, or tense mealtimes can activate stress responses that interfere with digestion and enjoyment.

Creating Regulation-Supportive Mealtimes

Environmental factors:

- Calm, predictable mealtime routines that help children know what to expect

- Comfortable seating that provides adequate support and allows children to focus on eating

- Appropriate lighting and sound levels that don't overwhelm sensitive nervous systems

- Family connection time that builds positive associations with meals

- Flexibility for children with specific sensory needs or feeding challenges

Food presentation strategies:

- Offering small portions to avoid overwhelming children

- Including at least one preferred food at each meal to ensure some nutrition

- Allowing children to serve themselves when developmentally appropriate

- Presenting new foods alongside familiar ones without pressure to try them

- Using child-friendly plates and utensils that make eating easier and more enjoyable

Family meal dynamics:

- Focusing on connection and conversation rather than food consumption

- Avoiding battles over specific foods or amounts eaten

- Trusting children's internal hunger and satiety cues

- Modeling healthy relationships with food and eating

- Creating pleasant associations with family mealtime

Car Ride Chaos and Confined Space Strategies

Car rides create unique regulation challenges because children are confined in a small space with limited movement options while often being expected to sit quietly for extended periods. Add factors like hunger, fatigue, boredom, or car sickness, and you have a recipe for dysregulation.

Why car rides trigger meltdowns:

Sensory challenges including motion sensitivity, confined space anxiety, or sensitivity to car sounds and smells.

Lack of movement when children need proprioceptive or vestibular input to maintain regulation.

Boredom or understimulation during long rides without engaging activities.

Sibling proximity creating conflicts when children can't get space from each other.

Parent stress about driving safety while managing dysregulated children in the backseat.

Regulation-Focused Car Strategies

Before the trip:

- Plan departure times around children's optimal regulation periods
- Pack regulation tools like snacks, water, comfort items, and sensory tools
- Set clear expectations about the trip length and planned stops
- Ensure children have used the bathroom and aren't hungry before leaving
- Prepare engaging activities appropriate for car use

During the ride:

- Use music, audiobooks, or games that engage without overstimulating

- Plan regular stops for movement and regulation breaks

- Address conflicts quickly before they escalate

- Stay calm and regulated yourself to provide co-regulation

- Be flexible about activities and strategies based on children's needs

For long trips:

- Schedule extra time for regulation breaks and unexpected needs

- Pack variety in activities and snacks to maintain engagement

- Consider splitting very long trips into manageable segments

- Plan overnight stops that allow for full nervous system recovery

- Maintain flexible expectations about arrival times and perfect behavior

Birthday Party Overwhelm and Special Event Planning

Birthday parties and special events often create perfect storms of dysregulation through overstimulation, social pressure, sugar consumption, disrupted routines, and high expectations for "fun" and "good behavior."

Special event regulation challenges:

Sensory overload from crowds, noise, decorations, and activity that can quickly overwhelm sensitive nervous systems.

Social demands that require sustained social interaction and performance of happiness or excitement.

Disrupted routines including meal timing, nap schedules, and familiar comfort items.

Sugar and food consumption that creates blood sugar spikes and crashes affecting regulation.

Excitement and anticipation that can push children into hyperarousal before events even begin.

Performance pressure to behave perfectly or have fun in prescribed ways.

Regulation-Smart Event Planning

Pre-event preparation:

- Discuss the event schedule and expectations in advance
- Plan arrival and departure times based on the child's optimal regulation windows
- Identify safe spaces or quiet areas where children can retreat if overwhelmed
- Pack regulation tools and comfort items in a small bag
- Eat a protein-rich snack before attending to stabilize blood sugar

During events:

- Monitor children's regulation levels and provide breaks as needed
- Stay nearby to offer co-regulation during overwhelming moments
- Allow early departure if children become dysregulated
- Focus on connection and enjoyment rather than perfect behavior
- Help children identify and communicate their needs

Post-event recovery:

- Plan quiet, calming activities after stimulating events

- Allow extra time for regulation recovery

- Process the experience together, celebrating successes and problem-solving challenges

- Return to normal routines as quickly as possible

- Be patient with temporary regression or increased sensitivity

Doctor and Dentist Visits

Medical visits combine multiple regulation challenges: unfamiliar environments, potential pain or discomfort, loss of control, and often anxiety about health or procedures. These factors can push even well-regulated children outside their window of tolerance.

Medical anxiety preparation strategies:

Advance preparation through books, videos, or social stories that explain what will happen during the visit.

Comfort items that provide sensory grounding and emotional support during stressful moments.

Advocacy with providers about the child's regulation needs and effective communication strategies.

Positioning and support that helps children feel safe and in control during examinations or procedures.

Distraction and coping tools like music, games, or breathing exercises that help children manage anxiety and discomfort.

Post-visit recovery plans that acknowledge the stress of medical visits and provide appropriate support for regulation recovery.

Working with Medical Providers

Many healthcare providers appreciate when families communicate about children's regulation needs and specific strategies that help during visits. Consider sharing:

- Your child's specific triggers or sensitivities
- Strategies that help them stay calm during examinations
- Communication styles that work best with your child
- Any accommodations that might be helpful
- Warning signs that your child is becoming overwhelmed

Building positive relationships with medical providers who understand children's regulation needs can make ongoing healthcare much easier for everyone involved.

Emergency Regulation Kit Contents

Having regulation tools readily available prevents minor dysregulation from escalating into major meltdowns. Every family's emergency kit will look different based on their children's specific needs and preferences.

Essential kit components might include:

Sensory tools:

- Fidget items for restless hands
- Noise-canceling headphones for auditory sensitivity
- Sunglasses for light sensitivity
- Weighted lap pad for calming pressure
- Essential oil roller for calming scents

Comfort items:

- Small stuffed animal or comfort object
- Family photo for connection when separated

- Soft blanket or piece of fabric for tactile comfort
- Favorite small book or visual support

Practical supplies:

- Healthy snacks for blood sugar stability
- Water bottle for hydration
- Tissues for tears or sensory needs
- Small notebook and crayons for expression
- Timer for managing transitions

Regulation activities:

- Breathing exercise cards with simple instructions
- Calm-down strategies written in child-friendly language
- Movement activities that can be done anywhere
- Grounding techniques using five senses
- Contact information for supportive adults

Kit Customization by Age and Need

Toddler kits focus on sensory comfort and distraction: soft toys, board books, crackers, sippy cup, and simple music.

Preschool kits might include emotional regulation tools: feeling cards, stress ball, small puzzle, healthy snacks, and comfort item.

School-age kits can include more sophisticated tools: journaling supplies, breathing exercise cards, fidget items, book, and calming music.

Teen kits might emphasize autonomy and choice: personal music device, journal, art supplies, favorite gum or mints, and stress management apps.

Scripts for Common Situations

Having prepared responses for common dysregulation scenarios helps parents stay calm and therapeutic even during stressful moments. These scripts address the nervous system needs underlying challenging behaviors.

Meltdown Response Scripts

When your child is in hyperarousal (tantrum, aggression, panic):

"I can see your body is having big feelings right now. You're safe. I'm going to stay right here with you until your body feels calmer."

"Your nervous system is working really hard right now. Let's help it settle down together."

"These feelings are really big and scary. I'm not scared of your big feelings, and I'm not going anywhere."

When your child is in hypoarousal (shutdown, withdrawal, dissociation):

"I notice you seem far away right now. I'm here when you're ready to connect."

"Sometimes our bodies need to rest when things feel too big. I'll stay nearby while you take the time you need."

"You don't have to talk right now. I just want you to know I'm here and you're safe."

Validation and Co-Regulation Scripts

For acknowledging difficult emotions:

"You're having a hard time right now, and that makes sense."

"These feelings are really big. Feelings this big can feel scary in your body."

"I believe you that this feels really hard for you right now."

For offering support:

"What does your body need right now to feel safer?"

"Would it help to take some deep breaths together?"

"I'm going to breathe slowly and calmly. You can breathe with me if that feels good."

These scripts work because they validate the child's experience while offering concrete support for nervous system regulation.

Environmental Quick Fixes

Small environmental changes can significantly expand children's windows of tolerance by reducing sensory triggers, increasing predictability, and supporting regulation throughout the day.

Lighting modifications:

- Use warm, soft lighting instead of bright fluorescent lights
- Provide lamp options so children can adjust lighting to their needs
- Install dimmer switches in key areas like bedrooms and playrooms
- Use natural light when possible, particularly in the morning

Sound management:

- Reduce background noise from TVs, radios, or household appliances
- Use white noise machines to mask unpredictable sounds
- Create quiet zones where children can retreat when overstimulated
- Consider noise-canceling headphones for particularly sensitive children

Organization and predictability:

- Use clear containers and labels so children know where things belong

- Create designated spaces for important items like backpacks and shoes

- Establish family command centers with schedules and important information

- Reduce visual clutter that can overwhelm sensitive children

Comfort and regulation spaces:

- Create cozy corners with soft textures and calming colors

- Provide regulation tools that are easily accessible when needed

- Ensure each child has private space for retreat and recovery

- Include nature elements like plants or natural materials when possible

Quick Environmental Assessments

When children struggle with regulation in specific spaces, consider:

- **Is the environment too stimulating or not stimulating enough?**

- **Are there hidden sensory triggers** like fluorescent light hum or air freshener scents?

- **Does the space feel safe and predictable** or chaotic and overwhelming?

- **Can children access regulation tools** when they need them?

- **Is there adequate space** for movement and retreat?

- **Are expectations clear** through visual or environmental cues?

Small adjustments often create dramatic improvements in children's ability to stay regulated in challenging environments.

When Nothing Works

Every parent faces moments when all their regulation strategies seem to fail and children remain dysregulated despite their best efforts. These moments don't mean you're failing—they're part of the normal process of learning to support your child's unique nervous system.

Reset strategies for overwhelming moments:

Change the environment by moving to a different room, going outside, or reducing sensory input in the current space.

Return to basics by focusing on immediate physical needs like hunger, thirst, fatigue, or bathroom needs that might be affecting regulation.

Reduce demands temporarily by eliminating non-essential expectations and focusing only on safety and connection.

Seek support by calling a trusted friend, family member, or professional who can provide perspective or practical help.

Take a break if possible, ensuring the child's safety while giving yourself a moment to regulate and regroup.

Try again later after both you and your child have had time to recover and restore your regulation resources.

When to Seek Additional Support

Some regulation challenges require professional intervention beyond what families can provide independently. Consider seeking help when:

- Dysregulation episodes are increasing in frequency, intensity, or duration

- Daily functioning is significantly impaired across multiple settings

- Family relationships are suffering due to chronic stress and conflict

- Parents experience secondary trauma or burnout symptoms

- School or community relationships are affected by regulation challenges

- Safety concerns arise related to aggression or self-harm

Professional support might include:

- Individual therapy for children to build regulation skills

- Family therapy to improve communication and relationship dynamics

- Occupational therapy for sensory processing support

- Medical evaluation for underlying health conditions affecting regulation

- Educational support for learning differences that impact behavior

- Parent coaching or support groups for caregiver needs

The goal isn't to eliminate all challenging moments but to build family capacity for managing them effectively while maintaining relationships and supporting each child's healthy development.

Making Daily Life Work for Every Nervous System

Daily dysregulation dilemmas are opportunities to support your child's nervous system development while building stronger family relationships and more effective coping strategies.

Morning meltdowns signal nervous systems that need gentle organization for the day ahead. Creating predictable, connection-focused morning routines helps children start each day within their window of tolerance.

Bedtime battles often reflect overstimulated nervous systems that haven't successfully transitioned to the calm state needed for sleep. Wind-down routines that reduce stimulation and increase connection support healthy sleep patterns.

Sibling conflicts happen when multiple nervous systems operate at different regulation levels. Understanding each child's unique window helps parents intervene therapeutically rather than just managing behavior.

Public meltdowns require portable regulation tools and understanding that children's behavior in public reflects their internal regulation state, not their character or your parenting effectiveness.

Homework resistance signals depleted regulation resources after demanding school days. After-school decompression and regulation support often resolve academic conflicts more effectively than increased pressure.

Screen time transitions challenge nervous systems accustomed to high stimulation. Thoughtful transition strategies help children move between digital and analog activities more smoothly.

Environmental modifications can significantly expand children's windows of tolerance by reducing triggers and supporting regulation throughout the day.

Emergency regulation kits and prepared scripts help families respond therapeutically to challenging moments even when stress levels are high.

Sometimes nothing works, and that's normal. Having reset strategies and knowing when to seek additional support prevents temporary setbacks from becoming long-term problems.

The goal isn't perfect behavior or elimination of all challenges—it's building family systems that support every member's nervous system needs while maintaining connection, growth, and joy in daily life.

Chapter 12: The Parent's Window

Your Regulation Matters Most

Rachel stared at the bathroom mirror at 11:30 PM, mascara streaked down her cheeks, hands still shaking from the evening's chaos. Her eight-year-old daughter Chloe had had a complete meltdown over homework, her five-year-old son Tyler had refused to stay in bed for the third time, and Rachel had lost it. Completely lost it.

She'd yelled. She'd said things she regretted. She'd sent both kids to their rooms and then collapsed on her kitchen floor, crying into a pile of unfolded laundry while wondering how other single parents made this look so easy.

"I'm supposed to be the grown-up," she whispered to her reflection. "I'm supposed to know how to handle this."

What Rachel didn't realize was that her own window of tolerance had been slowly shrinking for months. Between work stress, financial worries, and the daily demands of solo parenting, her nervous system was running on empty. She'd been giving everything to her children while neglecting her own regulation needs, and now she was paying the price.

Here's what nobody talks about in most parenting books: your regulation state affects your children more than any technique, strategy, or consequence system you could possibly implement. Children's nervous systems are constantly scanning their environment for safety cues, and the most important signal they receive comes from you.

When you're regulated, your children feel safe. When you're dysregulated, your children absorb that energy and become dysregulated themselves, no matter how hard they try to stay calm.

This isn't about being perfect. It's about understanding that **your nervous system is the foundation of your family's regulation,** and taking care of it isn't selfish—it's the most important thing you can do for your children's development and your family's wellbeing.

Why Parent Self-Regulation Is Non-Negotiable

The science is crystal clear: children's nervous systems are directly influenced by their caregivers' emotional states. Dr. Allan Schore's research on attachment and brain development shows that parents serve as external regulators for their children's developing nervous systems, particularly during the first few years of life (Schore, 2003).

Mirror neurons fire both when we perform actions and when we observe others performing the same actions. This means children literally mirror their parents' nervous system states through neurobiological mechanisms they can't control. When you're anxious, your child's brain activates anxiety pathways. When you're calm, their nervous system receives signals of safety.

The vagus nerve—the longest cranial nerve that connects the brain to major organs—plays a crucial role in this process. Dr. Stephen Porges's polyvagal theory explains how we constantly scan for safety or danger through unconscious detection of others' nervous system states (Porges, 2011). Children are especially sensitive to these signals from their primary caregivers.

This creates both challenge and opportunity. The challenge is that you can't hide your regulation state from your children—they feel it whether you express it verbally or not. The opportunity is that improving your own regulation directly improves your children's regulation capacity.

The Ripple Effect of Parent Dysregulation

When parents operate outside their window of tolerance, several predictable patterns emerge:

Emotional contagion spreads dysregulation throughout the family system. One parent's stress quickly becomes everyone's stress through unconscious nervous system communication.

Problem-solving abilities decrease as stress hormones interfere with prefrontal cortex functioning, making parents less creative and flexible in responding to challenges.

Patience and empathy diminish when the nervous system is focused on survival rather than connection, leading to harsher responses and damaged relationships.

Consistency becomes difficult as dysregulated parents struggle to access their values and long-term parenting goals during moment-to-moment interactions.

Recovery takes longer for both parent and child when multiple family members are dysregulated simultaneously.

Dr. John Gottman's research on family systems demonstrates that parents' emotional regulation skills are among the strongest predictors of children's emotional and behavioral outcomes (Gottman, 1997). This isn't about perfection—it's about developing awareness and skills for returning to regulation when you inevitably become overwhelmed.

Recognizing Your Own Triggers and Patterns

Most parents have specific situations, behaviors, or times of day that consistently push them outside their window of tolerance. These triggers often connect to unresolved experiences from our own childhoods, current stressors, or unmet needs that create vulnerability to dysregulation.

Common parental triggers include:

Defiance or disrespect that feels personal and activates our own childhood experiences with authority and control.

Repetitive behaviors like whining, arguing, or asking the same questions that overwhelm our sensory systems and patience reserves.

Time pressure situations where children's slower pace conflicts with adult schedules and responsibilities.

Public behavior that triggers shame, embarrassment, or fears about others' judgments of our parenting effectiveness.

Sibling conflicts that activate our own childhood experiences and fears about family harmony.

Bedtime and morning routines that compress multiple demands into short timeframes while everyone's regulation resources are limited.

Mapping Your Personal Trigger Profile

Understanding your specific trigger patterns helps you prepare for challenging moments and develop strategies for staying regulated when they occur.

Physical triggers might include:

- Fatigue from poor sleep or busy schedules
- Hunger or low blood sugar affecting emotional regulation
- Illness or chronic pain that reduces stress tolerance
- Hormonal fluctuations that affect mood and reactivity
- Sensory overload from noise, chaos, or overstimulation

Emotional triggers often connect to:

- Feeling overwhelmed by competing demands and responsibilities
- Fear of failing as a parent or not being "good enough"
- Sadness about your own childhood experiences or unmet needs

- Anger about unfairness or lack of support in your parenting role

- Anxiety about your children's future or current challenges

Situational triggers commonly include:

- Time pressure during transitions or daily routines

- Public settings where you feel judged or embarrassed

- Conflicts between children that feel chaotic or out of control

- Technology battles that seem to have no good solutions

- Discipline situations where you feel ineffective or lost

The goal isn't eliminating all triggers—that's impossible. Instead, awareness allows you to recognize when you're approaching your limits and implement strategies to stay within your window of tolerance or return to regulation quickly when you step outside it.

Healing Your Own Childhood Regulation Wounds

Many parenting triggers connect directly to unresolved experiences from our own childhoods. The way we were parented—both positive and negative experiences—creates neural pathways that influence how we respond to our own children, particularly during stressful moments.

Dr. Dan Hughes's research on attachment-focused parenting shows that parents who haven't processed their own childhood experiences often struggle to provide the emotional safety their children need (Hughes, 2009). This doesn't mean you need to have had perfect parents to be a good parent, but it does mean that unresolved childhood experiences can interfere with your ability to stay regulated during challenging parenting moments.

Common childhood experiences that affect adult regulation include:

Harsh punishment or criticism that taught us to fear making mistakes or to expect rejection when we struggle.

Emotional neglect that left us without models for healthy emotional expression or regulation.

Chaos or unpredictability that created hypervigilance and difficulty trusting that situations will remain stable.

Perfectionism or high expectations that taught us to view struggles as failures rather than normal parts of learning.

Lack of attunement from caregivers who were emotionally unavailable or overwhelmed themselves.

These experiences don't doom us to repeat unhealthy patterns with our own children, but they do require conscious attention and often professional support to heal.

Intergenerational Trauma Patterns

Trauma and dysregulation patterns often pass from generation to generation until someone in the family system develops awareness and works to change them. Dr. Mark Wolynn's research shows how family trauma affects parenting behaviors even when parents aren't consciously aware of the connections (Wolynn, 2016).

Breaking intergenerational cycles involves:

- Recognizing patterns that don't serve your family's current needs

- Understanding how your own childhood experiences influence your parenting reactions

- Developing new responses that align with your current values and goals

- Processing unresolved emotions and experiences through therapy or other healing modalities

- Creating new family traditions and patterns that support everyone's regulation needs

This work benefits not only you but also your children and future generations. When you heal your own regulation wounds, you prevent passing them on to your children and give them healthier models for managing stress and relationships.

Building Your Regulation Practice

Developing sustainable self-regulation skills requires intentional practice during calm moments, not just crisis management during overwhelm. Just as physical fitness requires regular exercise, emotional regulation requires consistent attention and skill-building.

Effective parent regulation practices share several characteristics:

Accessibility - They can be done quickly and easily during daily life without special equipment or lengthy time commitments.

Effectiveness - They actually impact your nervous system state rather than just providing temporary distraction.

Sustainability - They fit into your real life rather than requiring perfect conditions or unlimited time.

Personalization - They match your individual needs, preferences, and lifestyle rather than following generic recommendations.

Integration - They connect to your deeper values and long-term goals rather than feeling like additional tasks on your to-do list.

Daily Regulation Practices That Actually Work

Morning regulation routine (5-10 minutes): Start your day with intentional nervous system preparation through deep breathing, gentle movement, gratitude practice, or setting intentions for the day ahead.

Midday check-ins (2-3 minutes): Pause several times throughout the day to notice your regulation state and make small adjustments like drinking water, taking deep breaths, or stepping outside briefly.

Transition rituals (3-5 minutes): Create brief practices for shifting between roles (work to parent, daytime to evening) that help your nervous system adjust to different demands.

Evening wind-down (10-15 minutes): End your day with activities that signal to your nervous system that the day's work is complete and rest is coming.

These practices work because they're proactive rather than reactive. Building regulation capacity during calm moments gives you resources to draw on during challenging parenting situations.

Finding What Works for Your Life

The best regulation practice is one you'll actually use consistently. This means finding approaches that fit your personality, schedule, and preferences rather than forcing yourself into strategies that feel artificial or overwhelming.

For busy parents, micro-practices might work better than lengthy routines:

- Three deep breaths while your morning coffee brews
- Gratitude practice during your commute
- Brief stretching while children are occupied
- Mindful hand-washing that focuses on sensory experience
- Quick body scan while children nap or play quietly

For parents who enjoy structure, more formal practices might include:

- Morning meditation or yoga routine
- Daily journaling about regulation patterns and triggers

- Regular exercise schedule that prioritizes nervous system health

- Weekly therapy or coaching sessions focused on personal growth

- Monthly retreat or restoration time for deeper regulation work

The key is starting small and building gradually rather than attempting dramatic lifestyle changes that feel overwhelming and unsustainable.

Creating Support Systems

Parenting was never meant to be a solo endeavor, and parents who have strong support systems report better regulation, less stress, and more confidence in their parenting abilities. Dr. Brené Brown's research on vulnerability and connection shows that social support is one of the strongest predictors of resilience during challenging life periods (Brown, 2012).

Effective parent support systems include multiple types of relationships:

Practical support from people who can help with childcare, household tasks, or emergency needs when you're overwhelmed.

Emotional support from friends or family members who listen without judgment and provide perspective during difficult moments.

Informational support from other parents, professionals, or communities who share knowledge and strategies for common parenting challenges.

Social connection through friendships and activities that remind you of your identity beyond parenting roles.

Professional support from therapists, coaches, or other professionals who help you build skills and process difficult experiences.

Building Your Support Network

Many parents feel isolated and unsure how to build supportive relationships, particularly during busy parenting years when time and energy feel limited.

Start by identifying current relationships that could provide different types of support with better communication about your needs.

Look for parent communities that align with your values and parenting approach, whether through schools, religious organizations, neighborhood groups, or online communities.

Consider professional support even when things are going well, viewing therapy or coaching as maintenance rather than crisis intervention.

Prioritize relationships that feel supportive rather than depleting, and don't hesitate to limit time with people who increase your stress or judgment.

Practice asking for help with specific, small requests that allow people to support you without major commitments.

Rachel's support system transformation began when she joined a single parent support group at her daughter's school. Initially skeptical, she discovered other parents facing similar challenges and began building friendships that provided both practical help and emotional connection. She also started seeing a therapist who helped her process her own childhood experiences and develop better regulation strategies.

Self-Compassion When You Fail

Every parent has moments when they respond from dysregulation rather than their best intentions. These moments don't define your parenting or damage your children permanently, but how you handle them makes a significant difference in your family's overall emotional climate.

Dr. Kristin Neff's research on self-compassion shows that parents who treat themselves with kindness during difficult moments are more likely to model healthy emotional regulation for their children (Neff, 2011). Self-criticism and shame actually narrow your window of tolerance and make future regulation failures more likely.

Self-compassion involves three key components:

Self-kindness - Treating yourself with the same gentleness you would offer a good friend facing similar challenges.

Common humanity - Recognizing that struggle is part of the human experience, not evidence of personal failure.

Mindfulness - Observing your experiences without over-identification or dramatic storytelling about their meaning.

Repairing Relationships After Regulation Failures

When you respond to your children from dysregulation, repair is possible and often strengthens relationships by modeling accountability, emotional honesty, and the reality that all humans make mistakes.

Effective repair includes:

Taking responsibility for your own behavior without blaming your children for triggering you.

Acknowledging the impact of your dysregulation on your children's experience and emotions.

Sharing what you've learned about your triggers and what you'll do differently next time.

Reconnecting through physical affection, shared activities, or focused attention that rebuilds emotional safety.

Following through on changes you promise, demonstrating that your words have meaning.

Sample repair script: *"I made a mistake earlier when I yelled at you about your backpack. That was about my stress, not about you doing anything wrong. When I get overwhelmed, sometimes my body has big reactions before my brain can help me make good choices. I'm sorry that my big feelings were scary for you. You deserve a mom who stays calm even when things are hard."*

Rachel's Regulation Journey

Let me return to Rachel's story to show how parent regulation work unfolds in real life. After that difficult evening, Rachel realized she couldn't continue parenting from a place of constant overwhelm and stress.

Rachel's regulation transformation included several key elements:

Identifying her specific triggers through honest self-reflection about the situations, times, and stressors that consistently pushed her outside her window of tolerance.

Building awareness of her regulation patterns by noticing early warning signs of overwhelm before they escalated to complete dysregulation.

Creating proactive support strategies rather than just trying to manage crises after they occurred.

Addressing her own unresolved childhood experiences that were affecting her parenting responses.

Building a support network that provided both practical help and emotional connection.

Developing daily practices that maintained her regulation resources rather than depleting them.

Rachel's Daily Regulation Menu

Morning practice: Five minutes of deep breathing and intention-setting before children woke up, often with her coffee in the quiet kitchen.

Workday regulation: Brief text check-ins with supportive friends, walking meetings when possible, and mindful transitions between work tasks.

After-work transition: Ten minutes of music and movement in the car before going inside to reconnect with children.

Evening wind-down: Hot tea and journaling after children were asleep, processing the day's challenges and successes.

Weekend restoration: Longer activities like hiking, reading, or coffee dates with friends that provided deeper regulation and connection.

The key was making these practices sustainable rather than adding more pressure to her already full schedule. Small, consistent practices proved more effective than ambitious routines she couldn't maintain.

Daily Regulation Practice Menu

Building regulation capacity requires consistent practice, but the specific practices should match your personality, schedule, and preferences. Here's a menu of options to choose from rather than a prescription everyone should follow.

Physical Regulation Practices

Breathing techniques:

- Box breathing (4 counts in, 4 hold, 4 out, 4 hold)
- Physiological sighs (two inhales through nose, long exhale through mouth)
- Coherent breathing (5 seconds in, 5 seconds out)
- Belly breathing with one hand on chest, one on abdomen

Movement practices:

- Brief yoga flows designed for stress relief
- Walking meditation during daily activities
- Dance breaks to favorite music
- Progressive muscle relaxation
- Gentle stretching focused on tension areas

Sensory regulation:

- Cold water on face and wrists for activation
- Warm baths or showers for calming
- Essential oils that promote relaxation
- Weighted blankets or heat pads for comfort
- Nature sounds or calming music

Emotional Regulation Practices

Mindfulness activities:

- Brief body scans to notice tension and stress
- Mindful eating during meals or snacks
- Gratitude practice focusing on specific daily experiences
- Present-moment awareness using five senses
- Loving-kindness meditation for self and family

Cognitive practices:

- Journaling about triggers and patterns
- Reframing negative thoughts with more balanced perspectives
- Problem-solving specific challenges during calm moments

- Value clarification exercises that reconnect you with your priorities

- Self-compassion practices that reduce inner criticism

Connection activities:

- Brief check-ins with supportive friends or family

- Sharing challenges and successes with trusted others

- Asking for specific help when needed

- Participating in parent support groups or communities

- Professional therapy or coaching relationships

Trigger Reflection and Pattern Recognition

Developing awareness of your specific trigger patterns allows you to prepare for challenging situations and implement regulation strategies before complete overwhelm occurs.

The Trigger Reflection Process involves:

Situation identification: What specific circumstances consistently challenge your regulation (morning routines, homework time, sibling conflicts, bedtime, etc.)?

Physical awareness: What happens in your body when you're triggered (tension, shallow breathing, racing heart, clenched jaw, etc.)?

Emotional patterns: What emotions arise most frequently during triggering situations (anger, frustration, sadness, fear, overwhelm, etc.)?

Thought patterns: What stories do you tell yourself during these moments ("I'm a bad parent," "My children don't respect me," "I can't handle this," etc.)?

Historical connections: Do these situations connect to experiences from your own childhood or other significant life events?

Current stressors: What other factors might be reducing your regulation capacity (work stress, relationship issues, health concerns, financial worries, etc.)?

Using Pattern Awareness Proactively

Once you understand your trigger patterns, you can:

Plan ahead for situations you know will be challenging by building in extra support, reducing other stressors, or adjusting expectations.

Recognize early warning signs and implement regulation strategies before reaching your breaking point.

Communicate your needs to partners, family members, or support people who can help during vulnerable times.

Modify environments to reduce unnecessary stressors and triggers when possible.

Practice specific responses during calm moments so you have alternatives ready during triggering situations.

For example, if you know that morning routines trigger your overwhelm, you might:

- Prepare everything possible the night before
- Wake up 15 minutes earlier to have quiet regulation time
- Ask your partner to handle morning tasks when you're particularly stressed
- Create simplified morning routines that reduce decision-making demands
- Practice specific breathing techniques you can use during chaotic moments

Self-Care That Actually Works

Traditional self-care advice often feels impossible for busy parents because it assumes unlimited time, money, and childcare options that most families don't have. Effective parent self-care needs to be realistic, accessible, and genuinely restorative.

Micro self-care involves small practices throughout the day that support regulation:

- Mindful coffee drinking in the morning
- Deep breathing while folding laundry
- Gratitude practice during daily commutes
- Brief dance parties while cooking dinner
- Sensory pleasure like soft lotion or favorite scents

Daily self-care includes practices that fit into normal routines:

- Walking during children's activities instead of scrolling phones
- Reading during children's quiet time instead of doing chores
- Taking actual lunch breaks instead of working through them
- Going to bed at reasonable times instead of staying up for "me time"
- Choosing nourishing foods that support energy and mood

Weekly self-care involves slightly longer activities that provide deeper restoration:

- Coffee dates with friends who understand your life
- Solo activities like hiking, reading, or creative pursuits
- Professional services like therapy, massage, or healthcare

- Religious or spiritual practices that provide meaning and connection

- Hobby or interest pursuit that connects you with your pre-parent identity

Making Self-Care Sustainable

The key to sustainable self-care is integration rather than addition. Instead of adding more items to your already full schedule, look for ways to make existing activities more nourishing and restorative.

Transform necessary tasks:

- Make grocery shopping meditative by focusing on colors, textures, and choices

- Use driving time for calling supportive friends or listening to favorite music

- Turn household tasks into movement practice or mindfulness exercises

- Make bedtime routines connection time with partners or personal wind-down time

Protect existing restoration time:

- Notice activities that actually drain rather than restore you

- Set boundaries around social obligations that increase stress

- Limit news consumption or social media that affects your mood negatively

- Choose entertainment that genuinely relaxes rather than overstimulates

Rachel discovered that her most effective self-care involved:

- Morning coffee in silence before children woke up

- Walking during her lunch break instead of eating at her desk

- Weekly phone calls with her sister who lived across the country

- Monthly massage appointments she scheduled like important meetings

- Daily gratitude practice focusing on small moments of joy with her children

Repair and Reconnection After Difficult Moments

Every parent has moments when they respond from dysregulation rather than their best intentions. These moments don't define your parenting, but how you handle them significantly impacts your family's emotional climate and your children's developing relationship with mistakes and repair.

Effective repair serves multiple purposes:

- Models accountability and emotional honesty

- Rebuilds emotional safety after ruptures in connection

- Teaches children that relationships can survive conflict and mistakes

- Demonstrates healthy ways to handle personal failures

- Strengthens the parent-child relationship through vulnerability and authenticity

The Repair Process

Step 1: Self-regulation first Before attempting repair with your children, take time to return to your own window of tolerance through breathing, movement, or other strategies that help you access your prefrontal cortex and values.

Step 2: Take responsibility Own your behavior without blaming your children for triggering you. Use "I" statements that focus on your choices rather than their behavior.

Step 3: Acknowledge impact Recognize how your dysregulation affected your children's experience without minimizing or over-dramatizing the effects.

Step 4: Share learning Explain what you've learned about yourself and what you'll do differently next time, helping children understand that growth is possible.

Step 5: Reconnect Engage in connecting activities that rebuild emotional safety and demonstrate your continued love and commitment to the relationship.

Sample Repair Scripts for Common Situations

After yelling about homework: *"I made a mistake when I raised my voice about your math problems. That was about my own frustration, not about you needing help with math. I want homework time to feel safe for you to make mistakes and ask questions. Let's try again, and this time I'll keep my voice calm even if I'm feeling stressed."*

After impatient responses during bedtime: *"I didn't handle bedtime well tonight. When I feel tired and want the day to be over, sometimes I rush you instead of staying patient. Your bedtime should feel safe and connected, not rushed or stressful. Tomorrow night let's try again, and I'll remember that this time together matters more than finishing quickly."*

After losing patience during sibling conflicts: *"I didn't stay calm during your argument like I wanted to. When you two are upset, sometimes I feel overwhelmed and react too quickly instead of helping you solve the problem. You both deserve a mom who helps you work things out instead of adding more stress. Let's talk about what happened and figure out a better way to handle conflicts."*

Professional Support for Parents

Seeking professional support for your own regulation and emotional health benefits both you and your children. Many parents hesitate to prioritize their own therapy or counseling, viewing it as selfish or unnecessary, but research consistently shows that parent mental health directly affects child outcomes.

Types of professional support that help parents:

Individual therapy to process your own childhood experiences, develop regulation skills, and address mental health concerns like anxiety or depression.

Parent coaching focused specifically on developing parenting skills and strategies for managing challenging behaviors.

Couples or family therapy to improve communication, coordinate parenting approaches, and address relationship stressors that affect family regulation.

Support groups for parents facing similar challenges, providing both practical strategies and emotional validation.

Medical care for physical health issues that affect your energy, mood, and stress tolerance.

Finding the Right Professional Support

Look for providers who:

- Understand the connection between parent regulation and child behavior
- Use evidence-based approaches that have research support
- Respect your family's values and cultural background
- Provide practical strategies rather than just insight
- Help you build skills you can use in daily parenting situations
- Support your growth without judgment about past mistakes

Many parents find that even brief professional support can provide significant improvements in regulation skills and family dynamics. You don't need to be in crisis to benefit from professional guidance.

Partner Coordination and Regulation

When two parents are involved, coordinating regulation approaches and supporting each other's emotional needs becomes essential for family stability. Research shows that parental conflict and inconsistency create stress for children and can undermine even the best individual parenting efforts (Cummings & Davies, 2010).

Effective partner coordination involves:

Sharing regulation responsibility so one parent isn't always the "calm one" while the other struggles with dysregulation.

Communicating about triggers and needs so partners can provide support during vulnerable moments.

Developing consistent approaches to common challenges while respecting individual parenting styles.

Creating tag-team strategies for difficult situations where one parent takes over when the other becomes dysregulated.

Supporting each other's self-care and regulation practices rather than competing for limited time and resources.

Processing parenting challenges together in ways that strengthen your partnership rather than creating blame and conflict.

When Partners Have Different Regulation Styles

Differences in regulation styles can actually strengthen families when partners understand and appreciate each other's approaches rather than viewing them as right or wrong.

Some parents regulate through:

- **Activity and movement** - needing physical activity or task completion to feel calm

- **Quiet and stillness** - requiring reduced stimulation and peaceful environments

- **Social connection** - processing through conversation and relationship

- **Solo processing** - needing alone time to sort through emotions and thoughts

- **Structure and planning** - feeling calmer when systems and routines are in place

- **Flexibility and spontaneity** - thriving with variety and adaptive approaches

The key is supporting each other's regulation needs while coordinating your responses to children's needs. This might involve trading off who handles bedtime during stressful periods, creating individual self-care time for both partners, or developing signals that indicate when someone needs regulation support.

Technology and Parent Regulation

Our relationships with technology significantly impact our regulation capacity and our ability to provide present, attuned care for our children. Dr. Sherry Turkle's research on technology and relationships shows that constant connectivity can interfere with our ability to be fully present during family interactions (Turkle, 2011).

How technology affects parent regulation:

Constant stimulation from notifications, news, and social media can keep the nervous system in a chronically activated state.

Social comparison through curated social media posts can increase feelings of inadequacy and parenting anxiety.

Information overload about parenting strategies and child development can create analysis paralysis and self-doubt.

Reduced present-moment awareness during family time affects attunement and co-regulation capacity.

Sleep disruption from evening screen time affects next-day regulation and patience.

Regulation-Supporting Technology Habits

Intentional technology use that supports rather than undermines your regulation:

- **Scheduled check-ins** rather than constant connectivity

- **Curated content** that provides useful information without overwhelming you

- **Connection tools** that help you maintain supportive relationships

- **Learning resources** that build your parenting knowledge and confidence

- **Entertainment choices** that genuinely restore rather than overstimulate

Technology boundaries that protect regulation:

- Phone-free family meals and bedtimes

- Specific times for checking messages and social media

- News consumption limits that prevent overwhelm

- Evening wind-down without screens

- Morning routines that start with connection rather than information consumption

Creating Your Personal Regulation Plan

Effective parent regulation requires a personalized approach that accounts for your individual triggers, resources, and life circumstances. Generic advice rarely works long-term because it doesn't address your specific needs and challenges.

Your regulation plan should include:

Daily practices that build baseline regulation capacity through consistent, small actions that fit into your existing routines.

Trigger management strategies for situations you know will challenge your regulation, including preparation techniques and in-the-moment coping strategies.

Support activation processes for knowing when and how to access help from your support network.

Recovery protocols for returning to regulation after difficult moments and repairing relationships when necessary.

Growth goals that help you build regulation skills over time without overwhelming yourself with unrealistic expectations.

Adapting Your Plan Over Time

Your regulation needs will change as your children develop, life circumstances shift, and you build new skills. Effective regulation plans are flexible documents that adapt to your changing reality rather than rigid systems that add pressure.

Plan to review and adjust your regulation strategies:

- **Monthly** to assess what's working and what needs modification

- **Seasonally** as family rhythms change with school, work, and activity schedules

- **During transitions** like job changes, moves, or major family shifts

- **After difficult periods** to learn from challenges and strengthen your approaches

- **During growth periods** when you're ready to build new skills or try different strategies

The goal is building a sustainable system that supports your long-term wellbeing and parenting effectiveness rather than perfect adherence to any specific practice.

The Oxygen Mask Principle in Action

Flight attendants tell passengers to put on their own oxygen masks before helping others because you can't provide life-saving support if you're unconscious yourself. The same principle applies to family regulation—your nervous system stability is the foundation that makes everything else possible.

This doesn't mean becoming selfish or neglecting your children's needs. It means recognizing that taking care of your own regulation is taking care of your children because they depend on your nervous system state for their own sense of safety and stability.

When you prioritize your regulation:

- Your children feel safer and more secure

- Family conflicts decrease in frequency and intensity

- You model healthy stress management and self-care

- You have more patience and creativity for parenting challenges

- Your family develops healthier patterns around emotions and relationships

- Everyone in the family benefits from improved emotional climate

Rachel's family transformation began when she stopped viewing self-care as selfish and started understanding it as essential parenting work. As her regulation improved, her children's behavior improved not because she used better techniques but because they felt safer in her calmer presence.

Six months later, Rachel's home felt completely different. The same children in the same house with many of the same challenges, but now there was an underlying sense of calm and safety that made everything more manageable. Her children still had meltdowns, but they recovered more quickly. They still tested boundaries, but without the desperate edge that comes from feeling unsafe.

Most importantly, Rachel had learned that she could handle difficult parenting moments without losing herself. She'd discovered that regulation wasn't a luxury for parents with easy lives—it was a necessity for parents who wanted to show up as their best selves for their children.

Putting Your Own Oxygen Mask on First

Your regulation state forms the foundation of your family's emotional climate, making parent self-care an essential component of effective child-rearing rather than a luxury for parents with extra time and resources.

Parent self-regulation is non-negotiable because children's nervous systems constantly mirror and respond to their caregivers' emotional states. When you're regulated, your children feel safe. When you're dysregulated, they absorb that energy regardless of your parenting techniques.

Understanding your personal triggers and patterns allows you to prepare for challenging situations and implement regulation strategies before overwhelming moments occur. Awareness transforms reactive parenting into responsive parenting.

Healing your own childhood regulation wounds prevents unresolved experiences from interfering with your ability to provide the emotional safety your children need. Breaking intergenerational patterns benefits both current and future generations.

Building sustainable regulation practices through small, consistent actions proves more effective than dramatic lifestyle changes that feel overwhelming and unsustainable. The best practice is one you'll actually use regularly.

Creating strong support systems provides the practical help and emotional connection necessary for maintaining regulation during challenging parenting periods. Support isn't a sign of weakness—it's essential infrastructure for family wellbeing.

Self-compassion during regulation failures models healthy relationships with mistakes and strengthens family relationships through authentic repair and reconnection processes.

Professional support can provide valuable tools and perspective for building regulation skills and addressing factors that affect your parenting capacity. Therapy and coaching are maintenance, not crisis intervention.

Taking care of your own nervous system isn't selfish—it's the most important gift you can give your children. When you model regulation, resilience, and self-compassion, you teach these skills more effectively than any lecture or consequence system ever could.

Chapter 13: Building Family Resilience

Creating a Regulation-Friendly Home

Two years ago, the Martinez family was drowning. Parents Elena and Carlos felt like they were constantly putting out fires—nine-year-old Isabella's anxiety about school, six-year-old Diego's explosive tantrums, and three-year-old Sofia's sleep struggles that left everyone exhausted. Family dinners ended in tears, bedtime took hours, and weekends felt more stressful than weekdays.

Elena found herself yelling more than she ever thought possible. Carlos worked late to avoid the chaos at home. The children walked on eggshells, never knowing which version of their parents they'd encounter. Everyone was miserable, but nobody knew how to break the cycle.

The turning point came during what Elena now calls "the great meltdown of Tuesday." All three children were dysregulated simultaneously—Isabella anxious about a math test, Diego angry about having to turn off his video game, and Sofia overtired from a skipped nap. Elena and Carlos found themselves arguing about discipline strategies while the children spiraled further into chaos.

That night, after the children were finally asleep, Elena and Carlos sat in their kitchen and acknowledged the truth: **their family system was broken, and individual parenting strategies weren't enough to fix it.**

Fast forward to today. The Martinez house still has challenges—all families do—but there's an underlying sense of calm and connection that wasn't there before. The children still have big emotions, but they recover more quickly. Parents still feel stressed, but they have tools for returning to regulation. Most importantly, the family has developed collective resilience that helps them handle whatever life throws their way.

What changed wasn't just their parenting techniques—it was their entire approach to family life. They stopped thinking about behavior management and started thinking about nervous system support. They stopped fighting against their children's natural patterns and started working with them. They stopped trying to control outcomes and started building the foundation that makes positive outcomes possible.

The transformation didn't happen overnight, and it wasn't perfect. But by understanding families as interconnected nervous systems that influence each other constantly, the Martinez family created something beautiful: **a home where everyone's regulation needs are honored and supported.**

Family Systems and Collective Windows

Families are nervous systems within nervous systems, with each member's regulation state constantly influencing and being influenced by everyone else. Dr. Murray Bowen's family systems theory helps us understand that families develop patterns of interaction that either support or undermine individual regulation (Kerr & Bowen, 1988).

In regulation-focused family systems, several key patterns emerge:

Emotional contagion spreads both positive and negative regulation states throughout the family. One person's calm can help settle everyone, while one person's dysregulation can activate stress responses in other family members.

Regulation roles develop where different family members consistently serve different functions—one person might be the "calmer," another the "energizer," and another the "problem-solver."

Collective capacity for handling stress depends on the regulation resources available across all family members at any given moment.

Family rhythms develop around the collective window of tolerance, with certain times of day, activities, or situations consistently challenging or supporting the whole family's regulation.

Resilience patterns emerge where families either bounce back from challenges together or get stuck in cycles of dysregulation that persist over time.

Understanding Your Family's Collective Window

Every family has a unique collective window of tolerance that's influenced by individual members' regulation capacities, family stressors, environmental factors, and learned patterns of interaction.

Factors that expand family windows include:

- Strong relationships and emotional connection between family members

- Predictable routines and structures that support everyone's needs

- Effective communication patterns that address conflicts constructively

- Shared values and goals that create meaning and purpose

- Regular experiences of joy, fun, and positive connection

- Adequate resources for meeting basic needs and managing stress

Factors that narrow family windows include:

- Chronic stress from work, finances, health, or other external pressures

- Unresolved conflicts between family members

- Inconsistent routines or unpredictable daily patterns

- Individual regulation challenges that affect the whole system

- Isolation from supportive community connections

- Trauma or loss that impacts the family's sense of safety and stability

The goal isn't creating a perfect family but building awareness of your family's patterns and capacity so you can make informed decisions about activities, commitments, and responses to challenges.

Creating Regulation Rituals and Traditions

Rituals and traditions serve important regulatory functions by creating predictability, building connection, and establishing shared meaning that strengthens family bonds. Dr. William Doherty's research on family rituals shows that families with strong ritual patterns report higher satisfaction and resilience (Doherty, 1997).

Regulation-focused rituals differ from activity-focused traditions because they're specifically designed to support nervous system needs rather than just creating fun experiences.

Daily regulation rituals might include:

Morning connection time before the day's demands begin—perhaps snuggling in bed together, sharing breakfast quietly, or having brief individual check-ins with each child.

Transition rituals that help the family shift between different parts of the day, like welcome-home hugs after work and school, or brief gratitude sharing before dinner.

Bedtime regulation sequences that help everyone's nervous system prepare for sleep through consistent, calming activities that signal the end of the day.

Conflict resolution rituals that provide structured ways to address disagreements and repair relationships when conflicts occur.

Weekly and Monthly Family Rhythms

Longer-term rituals provide anticipation and stability that supports regulation over time:

Weekly family meetings that address logistics, celebrate successes, and solve problems together in a structured, democratic way.

Monthly special experiences that create positive anticipation and shared memories—these don't need to be expensive or elaborate, just meaningful to your family.

Seasonal traditions that help the family adjust to natural rhythms and transitions throughout the year.

Holiday approaches that prioritize connection and regulation over perfection or external expectations.

For the Martinez family, regulation rituals included morning dance parties in the kitchen, afternoon "connection snacks" when everyone returned home, evening gratitude circles during dinner, and weekend family hiking that provided movement and outdoor time for everyone.

Environmental Design for Nervous System Support

The physical environment significantly impacts family regulation through sensory input, organization systems, and the messages spaces send about calm versus chaos. Creating a regulation-friendly home doesn't require expensive renovations—it requires thoughtful attention to how spaces affect nervous systems.

Key environmental factors for family regulation:

Lighting choices that support different activities and times of day— bright, natural light for morning activation and warm, dim lighting for evening wind-down.

Sound management that reduces overwhelming noise while allowing for necessary family communication and activity.

Organization systems that reduce daily stress through clear storage, easy-to-maintain systems, and designated spaces for important items.

Comfort areas where family members can retreat for regulation when they feel overwhelmed or overstimulated.

Movement opportunities both indoors and outdoors that allow for physical regulation throughout the day.

Nature connections through plants, natural materials, or outdoor access that support nervous system calm.

Room-by-Room Regulation Support

Kitchen and dining areas:

- Calm lighting and reduced clutter during meal preparation and eating
- Comfortable seating that supports good posture and connection
- Organization systems that make meal preparation less stressful
- Space for family connection during food preparation and consumption

Living areas:

- Multiple seating options that accommodate different sensory needs
- Reduced visual clutter that can overwhelm sensitive family members
- Storage for regulation tools like weighted blankets, fidgets, or comfort items
- Flexible furniture arrangements that support both connection and individual space

Bedrooms:

- Individual sensory preferences honored through lighting, sound, and texture choices

- Calm, organized spaces that signal rest and safety

- Comfort items easily accessible for regulation support

- Privacy options that allow for individual retreat and recovery

Outdoor spaces:

- Access to nature and fresh air for nervous system reset

- Movement opportunities through play equipment, gardens, or open space

- Quiet areas for individual regulation alongside active play zones

Building a Regulation-Positive Family Culture

Family culture consists of the spoken and unspoken rules, values, and patterns that guide how family members interact with each other and respond to challenges. Regulation-positive cultures prioritize emotional safety, authentic communication, and collective support over perfection or external appearances.

Core elements of regulation-positive family cultures include:

Emotional authenticity where all feelings are acknowledged as valid information, even when behaviors need to be addressed.

Mistake recovery patterns that view errors as learning opportunities rather than failures, with repair and reconnection following conflicts.

Individual differences celebration that honors each family member's unique nervous system needs and contribution patterns.

Collective problem-solving approaches that include all family members in finding solutions to challenges that affect the family.

Support and cooperation as default responses to individual struggles, with family members helping each other succeed rather than competing.

Family Values That Support Regulation

Regulation-positive families often share certain values that guide their responses to both daily interactions and major challenges:

Connection over compliance - Prioritizing relationships and emotional safety over perfect behavior or immediate obedience.

Progress over perfection - Celebrating effort, growth, and learning rather than expecting flawless performance.

Authenticity over appearance - Valuing genuine expression and honest communication over looking good to others.

Cooperation over competition - Building family success through mutual support rather than individual achievement at others' expense.

Present-moment awareness over past regrets or future worries - Focusing on what's happening now and what can be influenced today.

Growth mindset approaches that view challenges as opportunities to build skills rather than threats to avoid.

These values show up in daily interactions through language choices, response patterns, and the stories families tell about themselves and their experiences.

Family Meeting Templates That Work

Regular family meetings provide structured opportunities for collective problem-solving, connection, and planning that supports everyone's regulation needs. Effective family meetings are brief, focused, and designed to build cooperation rather than impose adult authority.

Basic family meeting structure:

Opening connection (5 minutes) - Start with appreciation sharing, brief check-ins about how everyone is feeling, or other activities that build positive energy.

Logistics and planning (10 minutes) - Review the upcoming week's schedule, discuss any changes or special events, and coordinate family activities.

Problem-solving (10-15 minutes) - Address one specific challenge that affects the family, with everyone contributing ideas and helping develop solutions.

Fun planning (5 minutes) - Plan enjoyable family activities, special meals, or other positive experiences that everyone anticipates.

Closing ritual (5 minutes) - End with connection activities like group hugs, appreciation sharing, or brief games that leave everyone feeling positive.

Age-Appropriate Participation

Family meetings work best when all members can participate meaningfully according to their developmental capacities:

Toddlers and preschoolers can participate through picture sharing, simple choices between options, and physical connection activities.

School-age children can contribute ideas, help with planning, and take on appropriate responsibilities within the family system.

Teenagers benefit from having real voice and vote in family decisions, with meetings serving as practice for adult participation in democratic processes.

The key is structuring participation so everyone feels heard and valued while maintaining appropriate adult leadership for safety and major decisions.

Regulation-Friendly Home Audit

Assessing your current home environment for regulation support helps identify simple changes that can significantly improve your family's daily emotional climate.

Sensory environment assessment:

Lighting evaluation - Are there options for different lighting needs throughout the day? Can you reduce harsh fluorescent lighting or add warm lamp options?

Sound analysis - What are the noise levels during different activities? Are there quiet spaces available when family members need to retreat?

Visual organization - Does the visual environment feel calm and organized, or cluttered and overwhelming? Are important items easy to find?

Comfort and texture - Are there soft, comforting options available for family members who need tactile regulation support?

Temperature and air quality - Is the home comfortable for everyone, with good air circulation and appropriate temperature control?

Organization for Regulation Support

Organization systems that support regulation prioritize accessibility and maintenance ease over perfection:

Clear homes for important items like backpacks, shoes, keys, and homework supplies reduce daily stress and search time.

Visual organization using clear containers and labels helps family members find what they need independently.

Age-appropriate storage allows children to maintain their own spaces and belongings successfully.

Regulation tool accessibility ensures that comfort items, sensory tools, and coping resources are available when needed.

Simplified systems that can be maintained even during stressful periods prevent organization from becoming another source of family conflict.

Creating Family Regulation Rules

Family rules that support regulation differ from traditional behavioral rules because they focus on supporting everyone's nervous system needs rather than controlling specific behaviors.

Regulation-focused family rules might include:

"We help each other calm down" - Family members support each other's regulation rather than escalating conflicts or distress.

"All feelings are okay, but not all behaviors are okay" - Emotional authenticity is valued while maintaining safety and respect boundaries.

"We ask for what we need" - Family members are encouraged to communicate their regulation needs rather than expecting others to guess.

"We take breaks when we need them" - Individual retreat and recovery time is respected and supported.

"We solve problems together" - Challenges are addressed collaboratively rather than through punishment or individual blame.

"We celebrate effort and growth" - Progress and trying are valued as much as achievement and success.

Implementing Rules Collaboratively

Rules work best when family members participate in creating them rather than having them imposed by parents alone. This might involve:

Family discussions about what helps everyone feel safe, calm, and connected at home.

Problem-solving specific challenges that affect multiple family members and developing collaborative solutions.

Regular review and adjustment of rules based on how well they're working for everyone.

Natural consequences that connect to the rules' purposes rather than arbitrary punishments.

Modeling and support from parents who follow the same rules and help children develop the skills needed for success.

Extended Family and Community Integration

Regulation-friendly families often need to extend their approaches beyond the immediate household to include extended family, caregivers, and community members who interact regularly with children.

This integration might involve:

Educating grandparents and extended family about regulation approaches and your family's specific needs and strategies.

Coordinating with schools and childcare providers to ensure consistency across environments.

Building community connections with families who share similar values and approaches to child-rearing.

Advocating for regulation-friendly policies in community organizations, schools, and other systems that affect your family.

Creating reciprocal support with other families for childcare, emotional support, and practical assistance.

Handling Conflicting Approaches

Not everyone in your extended family or community will understand or support regulation-focused approaches. This requires careful boundary-setting and communication strategies that protect your family's wellbeing while maintaining important relationships.

Strategies for managing different approaches:

- Clear communication about your family's needs and non-negotiable boundaries

- Education about nervous system science when others are receptive

- Protective strategies when children will be in environments that don't support their regulation needs

- Respectful disagreement with relatives or community members who use different approaches

- Building alliances with supportive community members who share your values

The goal isn't converting everyone to your approach but creating enough consistency in your children's primary environments to support their regulation development.

The Martinez Family Transformation

Let me share more details about how the Martinez family created their regulation-friendly home culture over the course of two years.

Year One focused on building foundation:

Individual assessment helped Elena and Carlos understand each family member's unique regulation patterns, triggers, and needs.

Environmental modifications included creating quiet spaces for Isabella's anxiety, movement opportunities for Diego's high energy, and consistent sleep routines for Sofia.

Basic family routines were established around meals, bedtime, and transitions that supported everyone's regulation needs.

Parent regulation work involved Elena and Carlos each developing their own self-care practices and trigger awareness.

Professional support included family therapy sessions that taught communication skills and conflict resolution strategies.

School coordination ensured that Isabella's anxiety support and Diego's movement needs were addressed consistently across environments.

Year Two Brought Integration and Growth

Advanced strategies built on the foundation from year one:

Family meetings became weekly opportunities for connection, problem-solving, and planning that included all family members.

Conflict resolution skills were taught and practiced during calm moments, giving the family tools for addressing disagreements constructively.

Community building involved connecting with other families who shared similar approaches and values.

Extended family education helped grandparents and relatives understand the family's approaches and support them consistently.

Crisis planning prepared the family for handling major stressors like job changes, moves, or health challenges.

Celebration systems were established to acknowledge individual growth and family successes regularly.

The results were remarkable: School reports improved for all children, family conflicts decreased significantly, and Elena and Carlos reported feeling more confident and connected as parents. Most importantly, the children developed skills for self-regulation and conflict resolution that served them in all their relationships.

Daily Rhythms That Support Regulation

Regulation-friendly families often develop daily rhythms that support nervous system needs throughout natural energy cycles. These rhythms honor both individual and collective patterns while remaining flexible enough to accommodate changing needs.

Morning rhythms might include:

- Quiet waking time before family interaction begins
- Movement or sensory activities that help organize nervous systems for the day
- Connection rituals that build positive emotional tone
- Predictable routines that reduce decision-making fatigue
- Realistic timeframes that prevent rushed, stressful departures

Afternoon and evening rhythms often focus on:

- Transition support as family members return from work and school
- Decompression time for processing the day's experiences
- Physical activity or outdoor time that supports regulation
- Family connection through meals, conversations, or shared activities
- Individual retreat options for family members who need quiet recovery time

Weekend rhythms balance:

- Rest and recovery from the week's demands
- Family connection through shared activities and experiences
- Individual pursuits that support personal regulation needs
- Preparation for the upcoming week that reduces stress
- Flexibility and spontaneity that provides variety and fun

Adapting Rhythms to Family Needs

Effective family rhythms are responsive to changing needs rather than rigid systems that create additional stress:

Seasonal adjustments that account for changing light patterns, activity schedules, and energy levels.

Developmental changes as children grow and their regulation needs shift.

Life transitions like job changes, moves, or family structure changes that require temporary or permanent rhythm modifications.

Individual needs that might require accommodating one family member's regulation challenges or growth periods.

External pressures from school, work, or community commitments that affect family capacity and availability.

The Martinez family learned to adjust their rhythms based on school schedules, seasonal changes, and individual family member needs, always prioritizing connection and regulation over perfect adherence to any specific routine.

Celebration and Joy as Regulation Tools

Positive emotions are powerful nervous system regulators that often get overlooked in problem-focused parenting approaches. Dr. Barbara Fredrickson's research on positive emotions shows that joy, gratitude, love, and playfulness literally expand our capacity for handling stress and building resilience (Fredrickson, 2009).

Celebration serves multiple regulatory functions:

- Activates the parasympathetic nervous system associated with safety and connection
- Builds positive associations with family relationships and experiences

- Creates shared meaning and identity through collective joy

- Provides balance to the inevitable challenges and stresses of family life

- Strengthens emotional bonds that support regulation during difficult times

Effective family celebration involves:

Recognizing small victories rather than waiting for major achievements—effort, kindness, problem-solving, growth, and recovery all deserve acknowledgment.

Individual celebration styles that match each family member's preferences for recognition and appreciation.

Spontaneous joy through impromptu dance parties, surprise treats, or unexpected fun that brings lightness to daily routines.

Planned special experiences that give the family positive events to anticipate and enjoy together.

Gratitude practices that help family members notice and appreciate positive aspects of their daily experiences.

Making Celebration Accessible

Meaningful celebration doesn't require money, elaborate planning, or perfect circumstances. Some of the most powerful family celebrations involve:

- Acknowledging when someone tries something difficult, regardless of the outcome

- Sharing specific appreciations about each family member's contributions

- Creating photo displays or memory books that highlight positive family experiences

- Establishing special foods, songs, or activities associated with celebration

- Taking time to savor positive moments rather than rushing past them

The key is intentionality—consciously creating space for joy and appreciation rather than hoping they'll happen naturally amidst busy family schedules.

Building Collective Resilience

Resilient families aren't those who never face challenges—they're families who develop the capacity to navigate difficulties together while maintaining their essential bonds and recovering from setbacks effectively.

Family resilience involves several key capacities:

Stress tolerance that allows the family to function well even during challenging periods.

Adaptability that helps the family adjust to changing circumstances without losing their core stability.

Communication skills that allow family members to express needs, resolve conflicts, and support each other effectively.

Problem-solving abilities that help the family address challenges creatively and collaboratively.

Meaning-making that helps the family understand difficult experiences as opportunities for growth rather than just problems to endure.

Recovery patterns that help the family bounce back from setbacks and return to positive functioning.

Teaching Resilience Through Daily Experiences

Resilience develops through practice with manageable challenges rather than through lectures about being strong or tough. Families can build resilience by:

Modeling healthy responses to stress, disappointment, and conflict that show children how to handle difficulties constructively.

Processing challenges together by talking through problems, exploring solutions, and learning from both successes and failures.

Celebrating recovery and growth after difficult periods, helping children understand that struggles are temporary and manageable.

Building confidence through supporting children in facing appropriate challenges with adequate support and encouragement.

Creating family narratives that include both difficulties and strengths, helping children understand their family as capable and caring.

Preparing for Life's Challenges Together

Regulation-friendly families don't try to eliminate all stress from their children's lives—they prepare their children to handle stress effectively through building regulation skills, supportive relationships, and confidence in their ability to cope with difficulties.

Challenge preparation involves:

Age-appropriate discussions about life realities like disappointment, conflict, change, and loss that help children develop realistic expectations.

Skill-building during calm moments so children have tools available when they face difficulties.

Supported practice with manageable challenges that build confidence and competence gradually.

Family crisis planning that prepares everyone for how to handle major stressors like job loss, illness, or other significant life changes.

Community resource awareness so families know where to turn for help during overwhelming periods.

Resilience story development that helps children understand their family's capacity to handle difficulties together.

Crisis Preparation Without Fear Creation

Preparing for challenges requires balance between realistic preparation and maintaining children's sense of safety and optimism about the future.

Effective preparation:

- Focuses on building skills and resources rather than detailing potential problems

- Emphasizes family strength and support rather than individual vulnerability

- Provides concrete tools and strategies rather than abstract reassurance

- Maintains age-appropriate communication that doesn't overwhelm children with adult worries

- Builds confidence through supported practice rather than anxiety through dire warnings

The goal is helping children feel prepared and capable rather than fearful and overwhelmed about life's uncertainties.

Technology Integration for Family Regulation

Technology can either support or undermine family regulation depending on how it's integrated into daily life. Regulation-friendly families develop intentional approaches to technology that enhance connection and support nervous system health.

Regulation-supporting technology use:

Connection tools that help family members stay in touch and coordinate schedules effectively.

Learning resources that support both children's education and parents' skill development.

Calming applications that provide guided breathing, meditation, or other regulation support.

Organization systems that reduce daily stress through calendars, reminders, and planning tools.

Creative outlets that provide expression and enjoyment rather than passive consumption.

Family entertainment that brings people together rather than isolating them in individual activities.

Technology Boundaries for Regulation

Healthy technology boundaries protect family regulation and connection time:

Device-free zones during meals, family meetings, and bedtime routines that prioritize face-to-face connection.

Scheduled technology time rather than constant availability that prevents present-moment awareness.

Content guidelines that avoid overstimulating or upsetting material, particularly before sleep or during vulnerable times.

Co-viewing opportunities that turn screen time into connection time through shared experiences.

Digital sabbath periods that provide complete breaks from technology stress.

Modeling healthy relationships with technology that show children balanced approaches to digital tools.

Implementation Strategy

Creating a regulation-friendly family culture is a process that unfolds over months and years rather than a quick fix that solves all problems immediately. Sustainable change requires starting small, building on successes, and adjusting approaches based on what works for your specific family.

The 30-day family challenge approach:

Week 1: Focus on basic regulation awareness by helping all family members notice their own patterns and needs.

Week 2: Implement one simple daily rhythm that supports collective regulation, such as family check-ins or transition rituals.

Week 3: Address one specific challenge area (bedtime, morning routine, homework, etc.) using regulation-focused strategies.

Week 4: Add celebration and joy practices that build positive family experiences and emotional connections.

Months 2-3: Build on foundation successes by adding family meetings, environmental modifications, and extended family coordination.

Months 4-6: Develop crisis planning, resilience skills, and long-term growth strategies that prepare the family for ongoing success.

Tracking Progress and Adjusting Approaches

Family regulation development requires ongoing attention and adjustment based on what's working and what needs modification:

Weekly family reflection about what felt good and what felt challenging during the previous week.

Monthly assessment of family regulation patterns, conflict frequency, and overall emotional climate.

Seasonal planning that adjusts approaches based on changing schedules, developmental needs, and life circumstances.

Annual family visioning that helps the family set goals and priorities for continued growth and development.

The key is maintaining realistic expectations while building momentum through consistent, small improvements that accumulate over time.

Long-Term Vision for Regulation-Friendly Families

Families who successfully integrate regulation approaches often describe profound shifts not just in behavior management but in their entire experience of family life. These changes create positive cycles that support continued growth and resilience.

Long-term benefits typically include:

Improved family relationships with less conflict, more connection, and greater mutual support during challenges.

Individual skill development as family members build regulation, communication, and problem-solving abilities.

Increased confidence in handling whatever challenges life presents, knowing the family has tools and resources.

Positive family identity based on cooperation, growth, and mutual care rather than perfection or external achievement.

Community contribution as regulated families often become resources for other families facing similar challenges.

Intergenerational change that affects not just current family members but future generations who learn different patterns.

The Martinez family's transformation continues as the children develop into teenagers and young adults who understand their own regulation needs, communicate effectively, and handle stress with skills learned through years of family practice. Elena and Carlos report that parenting feels collaborative rather than combative, and family life includes joy and connection alongside the inevitable challenges.

Their home has become a place where everyone's nervous system can function optimally, creating the foundation for learning, growth, and authentic relationships that will serve all family members throughout their lives.

Creating Your Family's Regulation Foundation

Building family resilience through regulation-friendly approaches transforms not just individual behaviors but the entire emotional climate of family life, creating environments where everyone can thrive.

Family systems operate as interconnected nervous systems where each member's regulation state influences everyone else. Understanding these dynamics allows families to support collective wellbeing rather than just managing individual problems.

Regulation rituals and traditions provide predictability and connection that expand the family's collective window of tolerance. Daily, weekly, and seasonal rhythms support nervous system needs while building positive family identity.

Environmental design significantly impacts family regulation through sensory input, organization systems, and the messages physical spaces send about calm versus chaos. Thoughtful modifications support everyone's nervous system needs.

Regulation-positive family cultures prioritize emotional safety, authentic communication, and collective support over perfection or external appearances. These cultures are built through consistent daily interactions and shared values.

Family meetings and collaborative problem-solving teach democratic participation while addressing challenges that affect the whole family. Age-appropriate participation builds investment and skills.

Extended family and community integration ensures consistency across environments while building supportive networks that strengthen family resilience.

Celebration and joy serve important regulatory functions that balance the inevitable challenges of family life while building positive emotional connections.

Long-term implementation requires patience, flexibility, and commitment to growth over perfection. Small, consistent changes accumulate into profound family transformation over time.

The goal isn't creating a perfect family but building collective capacity for handling life's challenges while maintaining connection, joy, and authentic relationships that support everyone's growth and wellbeing.

Chapter 14: Building Lifetime Emotional Resilience

Five years ago, three families began their window of tolerance journeys from very different starting points. Today, their stories illustrate the profound long-term impact of nervous system-aware parenting—not just on behavior management, but on the fundamental trajectory of children's emotional development and family relationships.

The Chen family started when their seven-year-old daughter Amy was having daily meltdowns that seemed to come from nowhere. Traditional discipline approaches had failed, school was becoming a battleground, and parents Lisa and David were exhausted from walking on eggshells around Amy's explosive emotions.

The Johnson family began their journey when single father Marcus realized his ADHD son Tyler's "behavioral problems" were actually regulation challenges. After years of punishment-based approaches that only made things worse, Marcus was ready to try something completely different.

The Rodriguez family entered window work during a crisis when their formerly easy-going ten-year-old daughter Sofia developed severe anxiety after her grandmother's sudden death. Traditional therapy helped, but the family wanted tools for preventing future emotional crises.

Today, all three families look fundamentally different. Not because their children don't have big emotions or challenging moments—they do. But because these families have built emotional infrastructure that supports resilience, recovery, and authentic relationships that can weather any storm.

Here's what nobody tells you about the long game: window of tolerance parenting doesn't just change your child's behavior in the moment. It literally changes how their nervous system develops, how they approach relationships throughout life, and how they'll parent their own children someday.

This isn't hyperbole. The regulation skills, emotional intelligence, and nervous system awareness your children develop now become the foundation for their adult mental health, relationship success, and capacity to handle whatever challenges life presents.

From Crisis Management to Prevention

The most significant shift families experience as they develop window awareness is moving from reactive crisis management to proactive prevention and skill-building. Instead of constantly putting out fires, families learn to recognize early warning signs and create conditions that support ongoing regulation.

Amy Chen's transformation illustrates this progression. Initially, her parents' entire parenting strategy revolved around avoiding Amy's triggers and managing the aftermath of her meltdowns. They tiptoed around her emotional volatility, never knowing what might set off the next explosion.

Five years later, Amy still has intense emotions—that's part of her temperament—but she has tools for managing them. More importantly, her family has systems for supporting her regulation proactively rather than just responding to crises.

The prevention-focused approach includes:

Daily regulation practices that build baseline nervous system stability rather than waiting for problems to arise.

Environmental modifications that reduce unnecessary stressors and support optimal functioning for all family members.

Skill-building during calm moments when children can actually learn and practice new strategies rather than trying to teach during crises.

Early intervention strategies that address regulation challenges before they escalate to full dysregulation.

Family systems approaches that strengthen the entire family's capacity to support each other during challenging times.

The Neuroscience of Prevention

Dr. Dan Siegel's research on neuroplasticity shows that the repeated experiences we provide children literally shape their brain development (Siegel, 2020). When children regularly experience co-regulation, emotional validation, and effective coping strategies, these patterns become neurologically embedded as their default responses to stress.

Children who grow up with regulation support develop:

- **Stronger prefrontal cortex functioning** that supports executive function and emotional regulation throughout life

- **Healthier stress response systems** that activate appropriately and return to baseline more quickly

- **Better interoceptive awareness** that helps them recognize and respond to their own needs

- **More resilient attachment patterns** that support healthy relationships across the lifespan

- **Improved emotional intelligence** that serves them in academic, professional, and personal relationships

These neurological changes don't just affect childhood—they create the foundation for adult mental health and relationship success.

Building Emotional Intelligence Through Window Awareness

Emotional intelligence—the ability to recognize, understand, and manage emotions effectively—develops naturally when children grow up with window of tolerance awareness. Dr. Daniel Goleman's research shows that emotional intelligence is a stronger predictor of life success than IQ (Goleman, 1995).

Window-aware children develop several key emotional intelligence competencies:

Self-awareness through learning to recognize their own regulation states, triggers, and needs rather than being confused or overwhelmed by their emotional experiences.

Self-management by building a toolkit of regulation strategies that work for their individual nervous system and practicing these skills during both calm and challenging moments.

Social awareness by understanding that other people have different windows of tolerance and regulation needs, developing empathy and perspective-taking abilities.

Relationship management through learning to communicate their needs, support others' regulation, and maintain connections even during conflicts or disagreements.

The Integration of Thinking and Feeling

Traditional approaches often create false dichotomies between thinking and feeling, suggesting that emotions interfere with rational thought or that logic should override emotional responses. Window of tolerance parenting integrates these aspects of human experience.

Children learn that:

- Emotions provide important information that should be acknowledged and considered
- Rational thinking works best when the nervous system is regulated

- Both emotional and logical perspectives contribute to good decision-making

- Regulation strategies help access both emotional wisdom and cognitive clarity

- Conflicts between thinking and feeling often signal the need for regulation support

Tyler Johnson's development shows this integration beautifully. As a child with ADHD, Tyler used to feel like his emotions and impulses were out of control, leading to shame and behavioral problems. Through window work, he learned that his intense emotions were information about his nervous system needs, not character flaws to be eliminated.

Now fifteen, Tyler uses his emotional intensity as a strength in his passion for social justice advocacy. He's learned to channel his natural intensity into causes he cares about while using regulation skills to maintain relationships and academic success.

Preparing Children for Adult Self-Regulation

The ultimate goal of window of tolerance parenting is raising children who can regulate their own nervous systems effectively as they move into independence and adult responsibilities. This preparation happens gradually through scaffolded skill-building that transfers regulation responsibility from parents to children over time.

The progression typically follows this pattern:

Early childhood (ages 2-5): Parents provide extensive co-regulation while beginning to teach basic body awareness and simple coping strategies.

Middle childhood (ages 6-11): Children learn to recognize their own regulation states and use tools independently with adult support and guidance.

Adolescence (ages 12-18): Teenagers develop sophisticated regulation skills and begin applying them in peer relationships, academic challenges, and preparation for adult independence.

Young adulthood (ages 18-25): Young adults practice full self-regulation while maintaining supportive family relationships they can access when needed.

Building Internal Regulation Resources

Effective preparation for adult self-regulation involves developing both internal awareness and external skills:

Interoceptive development helps children tune into their body's signals about hunger, fatigue, stress, and emotional states, building the foundation for self-care throughout life.

Emotional vocabulary gives children language for their internal experiences, making it easier to communicate needs and seek appropriate support.

Coping strategy repertoires provide multiple options for managing stress, with children learning which strategies work best for different situations and regulation states.

Problem-solving frameworks teach children how to approach challenges systematically rather than feeling overwhelmed or helpless when difficulties arise.

Relationship skills including communication, boundary-setting, and conflict resolution that support healthy connections throughout life.

Stress management techniques that help children handle academic pressure, social challenges, and life transitions without becoming overwhelmed.

The Ripple Effect of Regulated Children

Children who grow up with window of tolerance awareness don't just benefit individually—they change the emotional climate of every system they enter. Schools, friend groups, and eventually workplaces and communities benefit from the presence of emotionally intelligent, well-regulated individuals.

Sofia Rodriguez's impact on her peer group demonstrates this ripple effect. After working through her anxiety following her grandmother's death, Sofia developed exceptional emotional awareness and empathy. She became the friend other children sought out during difficulties, naturally providing co-regulation and support to classmates facing their own challenges.

Regulated children often become:

- **Peer mediators** who help resolve conflicts between friends

- **Emotional support providers** for classmates experiencing difficulties

- **Leaders** who create inclusive, supportive group dynamics

- **Problem-solvers** who approach challenges creatively and persistently

- **Change agents** who advocate for emotional safety in schools and communities

- **Mentors** for younger children who need regulation support and guidance

This influence extends into adult relationships and professional environments. Adults who developed regulation skills as children often become the colleagues others turn to during workplace stress, the friends who provide stability during life transitions, and the partners who can maintain connection during relationship challenges.

Intergenerational Impact

Perhaps most significantly, children raised with window awareness often become parents who naturally prioritize their children's emotional development. They break cycles of generational trauma and dysregulation by providing their own children with the nervous system support they received.

Research on intergenerational transmission of parenting patterns shows that emotional regulation skills are passed down through families (Bridgett et al., 2015). Parents who understand their own nervous systems and can stay regulated during parenting challenges are more likely to raise children with similar capabilities.

This creates positive cycles where regulation-aware families influence their communities, and those communities become more supportive of other families seeking to prioritize emotional development and nervous system health.

Integration with Other Parenting Approaches

Window of tolerance parenting isn't a replacement for other evidence-based parenting approaches—it's a foundation that makes other strategies more effective. Understanding nervous system science enhances rather than contradicts most positive parenting methods.

Window awareness integrates beautifully with:

Positive discipline approaches by helping parents understand when children are capable of learning from consequences and when they need co-regulation support first.

Attachment-focused parenting by providing concrete tools for building secure relationships and responding to children's emotional needs.

Montessori and child-led learning by honoring children's natural developmental patterns and creating environments that support optimal functioning.

Conscious parenting by building parents' self-awareness and emotional regulation skills alongside child-focused strategies.

Collaborative problem-solving models by ensuring children are regulated enough to participate effectively in finding solutions to family challenges.

When to Combine Approaches

Different family situations may benefit from integrating window work with other specialized approaches:

Trauma-informed therapy for families healing from significant adverse experiences requires professional support alongside nervous system awareness.

Neurodevelopmental approaches for children with ADHD, autism, or learning differences benefit from combining accommodation strategies with regulation support.

Medical interventions for children with anxiety, depression, or other mental health conditions work more effectively when combined with nervous system-focused family strategies.

Educational support for children with learning challenges becomes more effective when regulation needs are addressed alongside academic interventions.

The key is using window awareness as the foundation that makes other approaches more accessible and effective rather than viewing it as competing with other evidence-based strategies.

Annual Window Growth Assessments

Tracking your family's regulation development over time helps maintain momentum, identify areas for continued growth, and celebrate progress that might otherwise go unnoticed in the day-to-day challenges of family life.

Annual assessments might include:

Individual regulation skill development for each family member, noting areas of growth and ongoing support needs.

Family system functioning including conflict resolution patterns, communication effectiveness, and collective stress management.

Environmental support effectiveness assessing which modifications and tools are most helpful and which might need adjustment.

Community and extended family relationships that either support or challenge your family's regulation-focused approaches.

Goal setting for the coming year that builds on current strengths while addressing areas where additional growth would benefit the family.

Tracking Meaningful Change

Effective assessment focuses on functional improvements rather than perfect behavior:

Recovery time from dysregulation episodes—are family members bouncing back more quickly from difficult moments?

Conflict resolution patterns—are disagreements being handled more constructively with less damage to relationships?

Stress management during challenging periods—how does the family handle illness, schedule changes, or external pressures?

Communication effectiveness—are family members expressing needs clearly and listening to each other respectfully?

Individual growth—are children developing self-awareness, empathy, and independence appropriate for their age?

Family connection—do family members enjoy spending time together and feel supported during difficulties?

The Chen family's five-year assessment revealed remarkable growth. Amy, now twelve, still has intense emotions but manages them with tools she's internalized. Her parents report that family conflicts are resolved more quickly, and Amy has become a leader among her peers in emotional intelligence and conflict resolution.

Transitioning to Teen and Adult Independence

The goal of window of tolerance parenting is raising children who can eventually regulate their own nervous systems effectively without constant external support. This transition happens gradually through scaffolded skill-building that transfers responsibility from parents to children over time.

The independence-building process involves:

Increasing self-awareness as children learn to recognize their own patterns, triggers, and needs without parental interpretation.

Expanding coping repertoires with children developing multiple strategies for different situations and regulation challenges.

Building decision-making skills through supported practice with increasingly complex choices and consequences.

Developing relationship skills that allow children to seek appropriate support while maintaining healthy independence.

Creating personal regulation practices that children can maintain independently as they move into adult responsibilities.

Supporting Adolescent Regulation Development

Teenagers need different regulation support as their brains undergo significant developmental changes and they begin preparing for adult independence:

Collaborative planning around academic, social, and personal challenges that respects their growing autonomy while providing adult wisdom and support.

Crisis planning that includes teenagers in developing strategies for managing overwhelming situations independently.

Relationship skills that help teenagers maintain healthy friendships and romantic relationships while managing their own regulation needs.

Stress management for academic pressure, social challenges, and future planning that can feel overwhelming during adolescence.

Identity development support that helps teenagers understand their own temperament, values, and goals while maintaining family connection.

Tyler Johnson's teenage years show this progression beautifully. Now fifteen, he advocates for his own needs at school, maintains friendships despite his ADHD challenges, and has clear goals for his future that build on his strengths while acknowledging his ongoing support needs.

Teaching Children to Teach Others

One of the most powerful indicators of internalized regulation skills is when children begin teaching these concepts to others. This might happen with siblings, friends, or even adults as children develop confidence in their understanding and application of nervous system science.

Children who've internalized window awareness often:

- Help younger siblings recognize and cope with big emotions
- Support friends during social conflicts or academic stress
- Explain regulation concepts to grandparents or other adults
- Advocate for emotional safety in school or community settings
- Become peer mediators or emotional support resources
- Share coping strategies that have worked for them

This teaching happens naturally when children have genuine understanding rather than just compliance with regulation strategies. They begin to see emotional intelligence as a valuable skill that can help others, not just a personal coping mechanism.

Building Regulation Mentorship

Many families find that older children become regulation mentors for younger siblings, creating positive family dynamics where everyone supports each other's emotional development.

Effective sibling mentorship includes:

- Older children modeling regulation strategies during their own challenging moments

- Teaching younger siblings specific tools like breathing techniques or calming activities

- Providing comfort and co-regulation when parents aren't immediately available

- Celebrating younger siblings' regulation successes and growth

- Advocating for family modifications that support everyone's needs

This mentorship benefits both children: younger children receive peer-level support that feels accessible, while older children reinforce their own learning and develop leadership and empathy skills.

Creating Regulation Legacy

Families who successfully integrate window awareness often become resources for their communities, sharing knowledge and support with other families facing similar challenges. This creates positive cycles where regulation-aware families strengthen their entire community's capacity for emotional health.

Regulation legacy might include:

Informal community support through playgroups, school communities, or neighborhood relationships where regulation approaches are shared naturally.

Formal leadership in parent education, school policy, or community mental health initiatives that prioritize emotional development.

Professional development for parents who pursue careers in education, mental health, or other fields where regulation awareness enhances their effectiveness.

Extended family influence that changes multi-generational patterns of emotional expression and relationship dynamics.

Community advocacy for policies and practices that support children's emotional development in schools, healthcare settings, and community organizations.

Preparing for College and Career Success

The regulation skills children develop during their formative years directly impact their success in higher education and professional environments. College counselors report that students' biggest challenges often center around emotional regulation, stress management, and relationship skills rather than academic preparedness.

Regulation-prepared students typically excel in:

Stress management during high-pressure academic periods, testing situations, and social challenges that overwhelm other students.

Relationship building with professors, advisors, and peers that creates supportive networks essential for college success.

Self-advocacy for academic accommodations, mental health support, or other resources they need to succeed.

Time management and organization that reflects good interoceptive awareness and realistic assessment of their own capacity and energy.

Conflict resolution in roommate relationships, group projects, and social situations that inevitably arise during college years.

Mental health maintenance through recognition of their own warning signs and proactive seeking of support when needed.

Career Readiness Through Regulation Skills

Employers increasingly value emotional intelligence and stress management skills as automation handles more technical tasks and human work requires collaboration, creativity, and adaptability.

Regulation-skilled adults often demonstrate:

- **Leadership abilities** that include emotional attunement and team support

- **Creativity and innovation** that flourish when nervous systems are optimally regulated

- **Resilience during setbacks** that allows for learning and adaptation rather than defeat

- **Communication skills** that build positive relationships with colleagues and clients

- **Stress management** that maintains performance during high-pressure periods

- **Ethical decision-making** that integrates emotional wisdom with logical analysis

Sofia Rodriguez, now fifteen, already shows these qualities as she prepares for college and career exploration. Her early anxiety work taught her to recognize stress signals and seek support proactively, skills that serve her well in academic pressure situations and leadership roles at school.

The Science of Lifelong Regulation Development

Nervous system development continues throughout life, with the capacity for building new regulation skills extending well into adulthood. Dr. Rick Hanson's research on neuroplasticity shows that the adult brain remains capable of developing new neural pathways through consistent practice (Hanson, 2013).

This means that:

- Children who start regulation work later can still develop significant skills

- Adults can model ongoing growth and development for their children

- Families can continue improving their regulation capacity over time

- Setbacks don't permanent damage to regulation development

- Professional support can enhance regulation development at any age

However, early intervention provides advantages because childhood brains are more plastic and because regulation skills compound over time. Children who develop nervous system awareness early have more years to practice and internalize these skills.

Regulation Skills as Life Insurance

Think of regulation development as emotional life insurance that protects children against the inevitable challenges they'll face as adults. Just as physical health habits developed in childhood affect lifelong wellness, emotional regulation skills provide protection against stress-related illness, relationship problems, and mental health challenges.

Research consistently shows that adults with good emotional regulation skills have:

- Lower rates of anxiety and depression

- More satisfying personal and professional relationships

- Better physical health outcomes

- Greater resilience during major life stressors

- Higher life satisfaction and sense of meaning

- More effective parenting skills with their own children

The investment you make in your child's regulation development now pays dividends throughout their entire life and affects the lives of people they'll influence, including their future children.

Advanced Family Regulation Strategies

As families become more sophisticated in their window awareness, they often develop advanced strategies that address complex regulation challenges and support continued growth.

Advanced strategies might include:

Multi-generational healing that addresses regulation patterns affecting grandparents, parents, and children simultaneously.

Community building with other regulation-aware families that creates supportive networks for children and parents.

Advocacy and education in schools and community organizations that creates more regulation-friendly environments for all children.

Professional development that allows parents to integrate regulation awareness into their careers and community contributions.

Crisis resilience planning that prepares families for major life challenges through regulation-focused preparation and support systems.

Teaching Regulation to Extended Family

Many families find that educating extended family members about regulation approaches strengthens support systems and reduces conflicts around different parenting philosophies.

Effective extended family education includes:

- Sharing basic nervous system science in accessible, non-threatening ways

- Explaining specific strategies that work for your children without criticizing others' approaches

- Requesting support for family rules and expectations during visits or childcare

- Providing resources for extended family members who want to learn more

- Setting clear boundaries when necessary while maintaining relationship connection

Marcus Johnson found that teaching Tyler's grandparents about ADHD and regulation transformed their relationship with their grandson. Instead of viewing Tyler's behaviors as disrespectful or attention-seeking, they learned to support his regulation needs and became powerful advocates for his success.

Future-Focused Planning and Preparation

Regulation-aware families often engage in long-term planning that considers how current skill-building will serve children throughout their development and into adult independence.

Life transition preparation includes:

Middle school transition planning that addresses increased academic and social demands while maintaining regulation support.

High school preparation that builds independence skills while ensuring adequate support systems remain available.

College readiness that includes both academic preparation and emotional regulation skills necessary for independent living.

Career exploration that considers how different professional environments might support or challenge individual regulation needs.

Relationship preparation that teaches skills for maintaining healthy romantic relationships and friendships throughout life.

Parenting preparation that helps young adults understand child development and regulation so they can provide healthy emotional environments for their own future children.

Building Regulation Skills Resume

Helping children recognize and articulate their regulation skills builds confidence and provides language for seeking appropriate support in academic and professional environments.

A regulation skills inventory might include:

- Self-awareness abilities and emotional intelligence
- Stress management strategies and resilience skills
- Communication and conflict resolution capabilities
- Leadership and peer support experience
- Adaptability and problem-solving strengths
- Empathy and social awareness development

These skills translate directly into college applications, job interviews, and life success in ways that traditional academic achievements alone cannot provide.

The Long-Term Vision

Five years from now, where do you want your family to be? Not in terms of perfect behavior or elimination of all challenges, but in terms of emotional capacity, relationship quality, and collective resilience.

Regulation-aware families often develop:

300

Authentic relationships where family members can be genuine with each other while maintaining mutual respect and support.

Effective communication patterns that address conflicts constructively and maintain connection even during disagreements.

Individual thriving as each family member develops their unique strengths while receiving support for their challenges.

Collective resilience that helps the family handle whatever life presents while maintaining their essential bonds and values.

Community contribution as family members use their regulation skills to support others and create positive change in their schools, workplaces, and communities.

Generational healing that breaks cycles of emotional dysfunction and creates healthier patterns for future generations.

Maintaining Long-Term Perspective

The daily reality of parenting can make it difficult to maintain focus on long-term goals, particularly when children are going through challenging developmental phases or when life stressors create immediate pressures.

Maintaining perspective involves:

- Regular reflection on your family's growth and progress over time

- Connection with other families further along in their regulation journey

- Professional support that provides encouragement and guidance during difficult periods

- Self-compassion during setbacks that recognizes progress as non-linear

- Celebration of small victories that acknowledge ongoing development

- Trust in the process even when outcomes aren't immediately visible

The three families featured in this chapter all experienced periods of doubt, setback, and frustration during their regulation journeys. What sustained them was faith in the long-term process and commitment to their children's emotional development rather than short-term behavioral compliance.

Where Families Are Now

The Chen family has become a resource for other families dealing with intense emotions and school challenges. Amy, now twelve, facilitates a peer support group for middle schoolers dealing with anxiety and has clear goals for high school that build on her emotional intelligence strengths.

The Johnson family has developed such effective strategies for supporting Tyler's ADHD that Marcus now provides informal coaching for other single parents. Tyler, fifteen, has become an advocate for neurodivergent students at his high school and plans to study education with a focus on alternative learning approaches.

The Rodriguez family transformed their experience with grief and anxiety into deeper family connection and community support. Sofia, now fifteen, volunteers with younger children who've experienced loss and is considering a career in counseling or social work.

All three families report:

- Significantly improved family relationships and reduced conflict

- Children who are more confident and emotionally intelligent than their peers

- Parents who feel more effective and less stressed in their parenting roles

- Family cultures that support everyone's growth and authentic expression

- Optimism about their children's future success and wellbeing

- Desire to share their learning with other families facing similar challenges

These families aren't perfect—no family is. They still have difficult days, ongoing challenges, and moments when regulation strategies don't work perfectly. But they have something invaluable: **the confidence that they can handle whatever comes next because they've built strong emotional foundations together.**

The window of tolerance framework gave them more than behavior management tools—it gave them a roadmap for lifelong emotional health and relationship success.

Conclusion: Your Family's Regulation Journey

You've reached the end of this book, but you're really at the beginning of something much larger: **a lifetime journey of supporting your family's emotional development and nervous system health.** The concepts you've learned aren't quick fixes or temporary strategies—they're foundational principles that will grow and adapt with your family through every stage of development.

Celebrating Progress Over Perfection

The most important thing to understand about window of tolerance parenting is that it's not about perfect implementation or elimination of all challenging moments. It's about building awareness, developing skills, and creating family cultures that support everyone's emotional development over the long term.

Progress in regulation work looks like:

- Faster recovery from difficult moments rather than prevention of all struggles

- Improved communication during conflicts rather than elimination of all disagreements

- Growing self-awareness in children rather than perfect emotional control

- Stronger family relationships rather than perfect behavior

- Increased confidence in handling challenges rather than avoidance of all stress

Every family's journey is unique because every family includes different nervous systems, challenges, strengths, and circumstances.

Your progress won't look exactly like the families featured in this book, and that's perfectly normal and expected.

What matters is the direction of change over time, not the speed of progress or comparison to other families. Small improvements in regulation capacity compound over months and years into significant transformations in family functioning and individual development.

The Continuing Journey of Nervous System Awareness

Understanding your family's nervous systems is not a destination but an ongoing process of learning, growth, and adaptation. As your children develop, face new challenges, and move through different life stages, their regulation needs will change, and your strategies will need to adapt accordingly.

This continuing journey includes:

Developmental transitions that bring new regulation challenges and opportunities for growth at every stage from toddlerhood through young adulthood.

Life changes like moves, job changes, family structure changes, or health challenges that require adaptive regulation strategies.

Seasonal rhythms that affect family energy, mood, and regulation patterns throughout the year.

Individual growth as each family member develops new strengths, interests, and support needs over time.

Community involvement that extends regulation awareness beyond your family to support others facing similar challenges.

Personal development as parents continue their own regulation skill-building and healing work alongside supporting their children.

Maintaining Momentum During Difficult Periods

Every family faces periods when regulation feels more challenging—during illness, major transitions, external stressors, or normal developmental phases that temporarily narrow windows of tolerance.

Maintaining momentum during these periods involves:

- Returning to basic strategies that have worked before

- Reducing expectations temporarily while maintaining connection

- Seeking additional support when needed without viewing this as failure

- Trusting the foundation you've built even when results aren't immediately visible

- Practicing self-compassion during temporary setbacks

- Maintaining long-term perspective about your family's growth trajectory

These difficult periods often become opportunities for deeper learning about your family's patterns and for building even stronger regulation skills that serve you in future challenges.

Your Next Steps Forward

Starting or continuing your family's regulation journey requires both commitment and patience with the process of nervous system development and family change.

Immediate next steps might include:

Choosing one specific area from this book to focus on first rather than trying to implement everything simultaneously.

Assessing your family's current regulation patterns through the tools and frameworks provided in various chapters.

Building your own regulation practices as the foundation for supporting your children's emotional development.

Seeking professional support if your family faces significant regulation challenges that require additional expertise.

Connecting with other regulation-focused families through online communities, local support groups, or educational organizations.

Continuing your learning through additional reading, training, or professional development in trauma-informed and regulation-focused approaches.

Building Your Family's Regulation Plan

Your family's regulation plan should be:

- **Realistic** for your current circumstances and resources

- **Personalized** to your family's specific needs and challenges

- **Flexible** enough to adapt as you learn and grow

- **Sustainable** over the long term rather than requiring perfect conditions

- **Collaborative** with input from all family members who can participate meaningfully

Start small, build gradually, and trust the process. The nervous system changes you're supporting in your children will serve them throughout their entire lives and affect every relationship they form, every challenge they face, and every contribution they make to their communities.

The Ripple Effect Continues

Your family's regulation journey extends far beyond your household. Children who grow up understanding their nervous systems become adults who prioritize emotional health in their relationships, workplaces, and communities. They become parents who naturally provide regulation support for their own children. They become friends, partners, and colleagues who contribute to emotional safety and resilience in all their relationships.

The investment you're making in your family's emotional development creates positive change that extends through generations and into every system your children will participate in throughout their lives.

This work matters. Your children's future emotional health matters. Your family's contribution to creating a more regulation-aware, emotionally intelligent world matters.

The window of tolerance framework provides a roadmap, but you provide the commitment, love, and daily attention that makes lasting change possible. Trust yourself, trust your children's capacity for growth, and trust that the small steps you take today are building the foundation for lifelong emotional resilience and authentic relationships.

Your family's regulation journey is just beginning, and the possibilities are extraordinary.

Building Your Family's Emotional Future

The window of tolerance framework provides more than behavior management strategies—it offers a roadmap for building lifetime emotional resilience that serves children throughout their development and into adult independence.

Long-term regulation development transforms children's neurological patterns, creating stronger prefrontal cortex functioning, healthier stress response systems, and improved emotional intelligence that benefits them throughout life.

Prevention-focused approaches move families from crisis management to proactive skill-building that addresses challenges before they escalate and builds capacity for handling future difficulties.

Emotional intelligence development through window awareness creates competencies in self-awareness, self-management, social awareness, and relationship management that predict life success more strongly than academic achievement.

Adult preparation happens gradually through scaffolded skill-building that transfers regulation responsibility from parents to children over time, creating confident, capable adults who can manage their own nervous systems effectively.

Ripple effects extend beyond individual families as regulated children become adults who contribute emotional intelligence and resilience to their communities, relationships, and future families.

Integration with other approaches enhances the effectiveness of evidence-based parenting strategies by providing nervous system foundations that make other techniques more accessible and successful.

Long-term family vision focuses on building authentic relationships, effective communication, individual thriving, collective resilience, and community contribution that benefit multiple generations.

The regulation skills your children develop now become their emotional life insurance, protecting them against stress, supporting their relationships, and enabling them to contribute positively to every system they enter throughout their lives.

Your family's regulation journey creates change that extends far beyond your household, contributing to a more emotionally intelligent and resilient world for everyone.

References

- **Adam, E. K., Hawkley, L. C., Kudielka, B. M., & Cacioppo, J. T. (2006).** Day-to-day dynamics of experience–cortisol associations in a population-based sample of older adults. *Proceedings of the National Academy of Sciences, 103*(45), 17058–17063.

- **Aron, E. N. (2002).** *The highly sensitive child: Helping our children thrive when the world overwhelms them.* Broadway Books.

- **Ayres, A. J. (2005).** *Sensory integration and the child: Understanding hidden sensory challenges* (25th anniversary ed.). Western Psychological Services.

- **Barkley, R. A. (2015).** *Attention-deficit hyperactivity disorder: A handbook for diagnosis and treatment* (4th ed.). Guilford Press.

- **Barlow, D. H. (2002).** *Anxiety and its disorders: The nature and treatment of anxiety and panic* (2nd ed.). Guilford Press.

- **Baumrind, D. (1991).** The influence of parenting style on adolescent competence and substance use. *Journal of Early Adolescence, 11*(1), 56–95.

- **Blair, C., & Diamond, A. (2008).** Biological processes in prevention and intervention: The promotion of self-regulation as a means of preventing school failure. *Development and Psychopathology, 20*(3), 899–911.

- **Bowlby, J. (1988).** *A secure base: Parent-child attachment and healthy human development.* Basic Books.

- **Bridgett, D. J., Burt, N. M., Edwards, E. S., & Deater-Deckard, K. (2015).** Intergenerational transmission of self-regulation: A multidisciplinary review and integrative conceptual framework. *Psychological Bulletin, 141*(3), 602–654.

- **Brown, B. (2012).** *Daring greatly: How the courage to be vulnerable transforms the way we live, love, parent, and lead.* Gotham Books.

- **Brown, T. E. (2013).** *A new understanding of ADHD in children and adults: Executive function impairments.* Routledge.

- **Carskadon, M. A., & Acebo, C. (2002).** Regulation of sleepiness in adolescents: Update, insights, and speculation. *Sleep, 25*(6), 606–614.

- **Carter, C. S. (2014).** Oxytocin pathways and the evolution of human behavior. *Annual Review of Psychology, 65*, 17–39.

- **Casey, B. J., Jones, R. M., & Hare, T. A. (2008).** The adolescent brain. *Annals of the New York Academy of Sciences, 1124*(1), 111–126.

- **Chang, A. M., Aeschbach, D., Duffy, J. F., & Czeisler, C. A. (2015).** Evening use of light-emitting eReaders negatively affects sleep, circadian timing, and next-morning alertness. *Proceedings of the National Academy of Sciences, 112*(4), 1232–1237.

- **Chein, J., Albert, D., O'Brien, L., Uckert, K., & Steinberg, L. (2011).** Peers increase adolescent risk taking by enhancing activity in the brain's reward circuitry. *Developmental Science, 14*(2), F1–F10.

- **Craig, A. D. (2015).** *How do you feel? An interoceptive moment with your neurobiological self.* Princeton University Press.

- **Cummings, E. M., & Davies, P. T. (2010).** *Marital conflict and children: An emotional security perspective.* Guilford Press.

- **Diamond, A. (2013).** Executive functions. *Annual Review of Psychology, 64*, 135–168.

- **Dishion, T. J., Nelson, S. E., & Bullock, B. M. (2004).** Premature adolescent autonomy: Parent disengagement and deviant peer process in the amplification of problem behaviour. *Journal of Adolescence, 27*(5), 515–530.

- **Doherty, W. J. (1997).** *The intentional family: How to build family ties in our modern world.* Addison-Wesley.

- **Eisenberger, N. I. (2012).** The pain of social disconnection: Examining the shared neural underpinnings of physical and social pain. *Nature Reviews Neuroscience, 13*(6), 421–434.

- **Erikson, E. H. (1968).** *Identity: Youth and crisis.* Norton.

- **Felitti, V. J., Anda, R. F., Nordenberg, D., Williamson, D. F., Spitz, A. M., Edwards, V., ... & Marks, J. S. (1998).** Relationship of childhood abuse and household dysfunction to many of the leading causes of death in adults: The Adverse Childhood Experiences (ACE) Study. *American Journal of Preventive Medicine, 14*(4), 245–258.

- **Fredrickson, B. L. (2009).** *Positivity: Top-notch research reveals the 3-to-1 ratio that will change your life.* Crown Publishers.

- **Garfinkel, S. N., Seth, A. K., Barrett, A. B., Suzuki, K., & Critchley, H. D. (2015).** Knowing your own heart: Distinguishing interoceptive accuracy from interoceptive awareness. *Biological Psychology, 104*, 65–74.

- **Goleman, D. (1995).** *Emotional intelligence: Why it can matter more than IQ.* Bantam Books.

- **Gottman, J. (1997).** *Raising an emotionally intelligent child.* Simon & Schuster.

- **Grandin, T. (2006).** *Thinking in pictures: My life with autism* (expanded ed.). Vintage Books.

- **Gray, P. (2013).** *Free to learn: Why unleashing the instinct to play will make our children happier, more self-reliant, and better students for life.* Basic Books.

- **Gunnar, M., & Quevedo, K. (2007).** The neurobiology of stress and development. *Annual Review of Psychology, 58,* 145–173.

- **Hanson, R. (2013).** *Hardwiring happiness: The new brain science of contentment, calm, and confidence.* Harmony Books.

- **Hirshkowitz, M., Whiton, K., Albert, S. M., Alessi, C., Bruni, O., DonCarlos, L., … & Adams Hillard, P. J. (2015).** National Sleep Foundation's sleep time duration recommendations: Methodology and results summary. *Sleep Health, 1*(1), 40–43.

- **Hughes, D. A. (2009).** *Attachment-focused parenting: Effective strategies to care for children.* W. W. Norton & Company.

- **Immordino-Yang, M. H., & Damasio, A. (2007).** We feel, therefore we learn: The relevance of affective and social neuroscience to education. *Mind, Brain, and Education, 1*(1), 3–10.

- **Jensen, F. E. (2015).** *The teenage brain: A neuroscientist's survival guide to raising adolescents and young adults.* Harper.

- **Kendall, P. C. (2012).** *Child and adolescent therapy: Cognitive-behavioral procedures* (4th ed.). Guilford Press.

- **Kerr, M. E., & Bowen, M. (1988).** *Family evaluation: An approach based on Bowen theory.* W. W. Norton & Company.

- **Kuypers, L. M. (2011).** *The zones of regulation: A curriculum designed to foster self-regulation and emotional control.* Think Social Publishing.

- **Lembke, A. (2021).** *Dopamine nation: Finding balance in the age of indulgence.* Dutton.

- **Linehan, M. M. (2014).** *DBT Skills Training Manual* (2nd ed.). Guilford Press.

- **Livingstone, S. (2008).** Taking risky opportunities in youthful content creation: Teenagers' use of social networking sites for intimacy, privacy and self-expression. *New Media & Society, 10*(3), 393–411.

- **Matsumoto, D., & Hwang, H. S. (2012).** Culture and emotion: The integration of biological and cultural contributions. *Journal of Cross-Cultural Psychology, 43*(1), 91–118.

- **Meltzer, L. J., & Mindell, J. A. (2014).** Systematic review and meta-analysis of behavioural interventions for paediatric insomnia. *Journal of Pediatric Psychology, 39*(8), 932–948.

- **Neff, K. D. (2011).** *Self-compassion: The proven power of being kind to yourself.* William Morrow Paperbacks.

- **Ogden, P., & Fisher, J. (2015).** *Sensorimotor psychotherapy: Interventions for trauma and attachment.* W. W. Norton & Company.

- **Perry, B. D. (2006).** Applying principles of neurodevelopment to clinical work with maltreated and traumatised children: The neurosequential model of therapeutics. In N. B. Webb (Ed.), *Working with traumatised youth in child welfare* (pp. 27–52). Guilford Press.

- **Porges, S. W. (2011).** *The polyvagal theory: Neurophysiological foundations of emotions, attachment, communication, and self-regulation.* W. W. Norton & Company.

- **Prizant, B. M. (2015).** *Uniquely human: A different way of seeing autism.* Simon & Schuster.

- **Ratey, J. J., & Hagerman, E. (2008).** *Spark: The revolutionary new science of exercise and the brain.* Little, Brown and Company.

- **Rizzolatti, G., & Craighero, L. (2004).** The mirror-neuron system. *Annual Review of Neuroscience, 27,* 169–192.

- **Romeo, R. D. (2010).** Adolescence: A central event in shaping stress reactivity. *Developmental Psychobiology, 52*(3), 244–253.

- **Schaaf, R. C., & Lane, A. E. (2015).** Toward a best-practice protocol for assessment of sensory features in ASD. *Journal of Autism and Developmental Disorders, 45*(5), 1380–1395.

- **Schore, A. N. (2003).** *Affect regulation and the repair of the self.* W. W. Norton & Company.

- **Siegel, D. J. (2012).** *The developing mind: How relationships and the brain interact to shape who we are* (2nd ed.). Guilford Press.

- **Siegel, D. J. (2020).** *The developing mind: How relationships and the brain interact to shape who we are* (3rd ed.). Guilford Press.

- **Singer, J. (1999).** Why can't you be normal for once in your life? From a problem with no name to the emergence of a new category of difference. In M. Corker & S. French (Eds.), *Disability discourse* (pp. 59–67). Open University Press.

- **Steinberg, L. (2013).** The influence of neuroscience on US Supreme Court decisions about adolescents' criminal culpability. *Nature Reviews Neuroscience, 14*(7), 513–518.

- **Thomas, A., & Chess, S. (1977).** *Temperament and development.* Brunner/Mazel.

- **Turkle, S. (2011).** *Alone together: Why we expect more from technology and less from each other.* Basic Books.

- **Twenge, J. M., & Campbell, W. K. (2018).** Associations between screen time and lower psychological well-being among children and adolescents: Evidence from a large-scale cross-sectional study. *Pediatrics, 141*(4), e20173826.

- **van der Kolk, B. A. (2014).** *The body keeps the score: Brain, mind, and body in the healing of trauma.* Viking.

- **Walkup, J. T., Albano, A. M., Piacentini, J., Birmaher, B., Compton, S. N., Sherrill, J. T., … & Iyengar, S. (2008).** Cognitive behavioural therapy, sertraline, or a combination in childhood anxiety. *New England Journal of Medicine, 359*(26), 2753–2766.

- **Weissbluth, M. (2005).** *Healthy sleep habits, happy child.* Ballantine Books.

- **Wolynn, M. (2016).** *It didn't start with you: How inherited family trauma shapes who we are and how to end the cycle.* Viking.

- **Zelazo, P. D., Müller, U., Frye, D., & Marcovitch, S. (2003).** The development of executive function in early childhood. *Monographs of the Society for Research in Child Development, 68*(3), vii–137.

- **Zero to Three. (2016).** *DC:0–5: Diagnostic classification of mental health and developmental disorders of infancy and early childhood.* Zero to Three Press.

- **Zuckerman, M. (1994).** *Behavioral expressions and biosocial bases of sensation seeking.* Cambridge University Press.

www.ingramcontent.com/pod-product-compliance
Lightning Source LLC
Chambersburg PA
CBHW070340090426
42733CB00009B/1240